Writing to Learn

Writing to Learn looks at how poetry can be used as an enjoyable way to teach literacy across the primary curriculum. It includes examples of poems and stories by children and clear descriptions of how to teach creatively within the framework of the National Literacy Strategy.

This book includes:

- cross-curricular approaches with sections on poetry and science; poetry and personal, social and moral education; poetry and art and music; poetry and religious education
- advice on different ways children can compose their writing and how computers can be a valuable aid to children's writing
- examples of published poetry and how it can be used to stimulate good writing
- advice on bringing writers into schools and publishing school anthologies

This book will prove invaluable to teachers and parents keen to teach writing who see children as active and critical learners. It shows that if we expect great things in writing from children, we get them.

Fred Sedgwick has many years of experience as a teacher and is now a freelance lecturer and writer. He is the author of a number of books on primary education, including *Read my Mind* (1997), *Thinking about Literacy* (1999) and *Shakespeare and the Young Writer* (1999), all published by Routledge. His poetry for children has been widely anthologized.

Writing to Learn

Poetry and literacy across the
primary curriculum

Fred Sedgwick

London and New York

First published 2000 by RoutledgeFalmer
11 New Fetter Lane, London EC4P 4EE

Simultaneously published in the USA and Canada
by RoutledgeFalmer
29 West 35th Street, New York, NY 10001

RoutledgeFalmer is an imprint of the Taylor & Francis Group

© 2000 Fred Sedgwick

Typeset in Goudy by Bookcraft Ltd, Stroud, Gloucestershire
Printed and bound in Great Britain by Biddles Ltd, Guildford and King's Lynn

British Library Cataloguing in Publication Data
A catalogue record for this book is available from the British Library

Library of Congress Cataloging-in-Publication Data
Sedgwick, Fred.
    Writing to learn: poetry and literacy across the primary curriculum /
    Fred Sedgwick.
       p. cm.
    Includes bibliographical references and index.
    ISBN 0–415–22413–6 (alk. paper) – ISBN 0–415–22414–4 (pbk.:
    alk. paper)
    1. Poetry – Study and teaching (Elementary)   2. Poetry – Authorship
    – Study and teaching (Elementary)   3. Language experience approach
    in education.   I. Title.
    LB 1576 S343413 2000
    372.64–dc21   00–030828

ISBN 0–415–22414–4 (pbk)
ISBN 0–415–22413–6 (hbk)

Dedicatory poem (for ER)

There's a place
  that, lucky,
    I get to
      sometimes. It
       separates
        ignorance
         and a partial
          understanding.
           Loneliness
            waits there, of
             course; an austere
             music; and
              a path of words
              printed
               without hope
              across a
               cold field.

'To write is to learn. Writing without learning is mere ornament, and collects dust'
Emily Roeves

'… poetic truth is metaphysical truth, and physical truth which is not in conformity to it should be considered false'
Giambattista Vico *The New Science* (1725)

Contents

List of illustrations		ix
Acknowledgements		xi
The principles		xiii
Introduction		xv

PART I
Poetry and science — 1

1	Observing the human body	3
2	Fruit, vegetables and other natural things	20
3	Bicycles and other machines	28
4	Cats and other animals	39
	Prose interlude: Children and their names	59

PART II
Poetry and Personal, Social and Moral Education — 73

| 5 | Me and the rest of the world | 75 |
| 6 | Lists | 90 |

PART III
Putting art in prison to set it free — 109

7	Pattern	111
8	Using visual images	119
9	Art and multicultural education	129
10	Poetry for its own sake	139
	Prose interlude: Short stories, and beginning a novel	158
11	'So help me God': Poetry and religious education	163

Appendices   179
    1 Bringing living poets into the classroom   181
    2 A word about learning by heart   186
    3 A selective glossary of terms useful in teaching writing   191
A list of poems used in this book to help children to write   199
References   201
Index   205

Illustrations

1	Eye – children's drawing and writing	13
2	I'll follow you – children's drawing and writing	18
3	Children and bikes (1)	29
4	Children and bikes (2)	29
5	Child's scribbles	30
6	Child's drawing of a bike (1)	31
7	Child's drawing of a bike (2)	31
8	Child's drawing of a bike (3)	32
9	Child's drawing of a cat (1)	43
10	Child's drawing of a cat (2)	43
11	Child's drawing of a cat (3)	44
12	Child's drawing of a cat (4)	44
13	My name – child's writing	69
14	Child's angry face	82
15	A totem-like figure	131
16	A story chair	133
17	A female head	134
18	Janus heads	136
19	Child's drawing of Janus heads	136
20	Benin bronzes	137
21	Child's drawing of Benin bronzes	137

Acknowledgements

Acknowledgements are due to the following schools:

All Saints' Primary, Bishops Stortford, Hertfordshire

Astley Cooper Comprehensive, Hemel Hempstead, Hertfordshire, especially Nannette Street, and the teachers on courses that she and her colleagues have run there for older junior children in the summer holidays

Bedwell Primary, Stevenage, Hertfordshire

Bushey Manor Junior, Watford, Hertfordshire

Castle Hill Infants, Ipswich, Suffolk

Charsfield Primary, Suffolk

Cherry Trees Montessori, Risby, near Bury St Edmunds, Suffolk

Combs First, Stowmarket, Suffolk

East Bergholt Primary, Suffolk

Featherstone Wood Primary, Stevenage, Hertfordshire

Foxborough Primary, Langley, Berkshire

Herringham Junior, Chadwell St Mary, Essex

Heybridge Primary, Essex, especially Sophie Chipperfield (thank you for the 'There is in me … ' poems, and the poems about animals, and much else)

Holy Rood Infants, Watford, Hertfordshire

Inkpen County Primary, West Berkshire

Ipswich Preparatory, Suffolk

Mary Exton Primary, Hitchin, Hertfordshire

Melton County Primary, Woodbridge, Suffolk, especially Jenny Allan

Nascot Wood Junior, Watford, Hertfordshire

Pearse House Courses

Radburn Primary, Letchworth, Hertfordshire

Reedham Primary, Norwich

St Laurence's Primary, Cambridge, especially Chris Wardle and Brigida Martino

St Margaret's Primary, Ipswich, especially Julie Taplin (thank you for the mirror poems)

Shildon Primary, Co. Durham

Tacolneston Primary, Norwich

Tattingstone Primary, Ipswich, Suffolk

Tuckswood First, Norwich
Vange Primary, Basildon, Essex
Wheatfields Primary, St Albans, Hertfordshire

Some paragraphs of this book originally appeared in *Montessori International*, edited by Paul Ryan. Others appeared in *The Poetry Book for Primary Schools* (ed. Anthony Wilson with Sian Hughes) published by The Poetry Society. My poems included here have appeared in the following publications: *Spokes* (Winter 1992), *Pizza, Curry, Fish and Chips* (Longman 1994).

Acknowledgements are due to the editors.

Thank you to Eloise Roberts, who sent me poems included here. Thank you to Dawn, who took some of the photographs.

All unacknowledged poems are my own.

The principles

There are seven principles about children, writing and learning that underpin everything in this book. They are:

- Observation: look, look and look again. They should also 'listen, listen, listen again'. And they should use the other senses in a similarly intense way.
- Children should be discouraged from immediate response. Putting their hands up without thinking, or with only rudimentary thinking, is merely competition, and nothing to do with what this book is about – that is, writing and learning. Similarly, their first response in writing is not usually the final, or the best, one. All writing takes more than one draft.
- The visual images that children make feed into their words and vice versa: their words feed into their pictures. Thus, drawing and other experiences in the visual arts should not be separated from thinking, feeling and writing.
- Writing – poetry and prose – is a democratic subject: it is not just for God's golden children. I do not mean by this that everyone's poems or stories are as good as everyone else's 'as long as they are sincere'. That is not true: it is a dangerous, sentimental delusion. But everyone has something to learn through the rigours of poetry, in particular. And in poetry there is essentially no competition.
- Make it new. This was Ezra Pound's dictum, and I break his rule here by saying it again. There is no point in repeating tired old phrases, or even lively ones, if they have been written before.
- The secretarial and the compositional are separate things, and should not be confused in our teaching. Of course children must learn how to spell, punctuate and use grammar conventionally. But while they are composing, they should not be tripped up by obsessions with these things.
- There is more than one way to compose. For example, you can write by hand, dictate to a friend, a teacher or a tape recorder, memorize, or type on a word processor. All good English schemes will offer children each of these experiences.

Introduction

Language and poetry as teachers of the whole curriculum

There are thousands upon thousands of books about children. Few of them, regrettably, are by children or even feature much of their writing. There are thousands of books on teaching literacy. These books rarely have anything to do with children at all. A significant few are about teaching poetry. Children do, occasionally, feature in them. One of these books is my own, *Read My Mind* (1997), in which I have developed a theory based on my practice in hundreds of schools. It can be stated simply like this: when children write poetry, they learn about four areas of knowledge:

- themselves,
- their environments,
- the relationship between themselves and their environments,
- their language.

I am going to leave the first area to emerge in the course of this book. I will, though, introduce the second and third areas here. They mean everything, from the natural, through the artificial, to the human surroundings of the writer. In curricular terms, this takes us from biology, botany and zoology, through physics and geography, to history and sociology.

The fourth area encompasses all aspects of what is now called literacy. This is a subject that, in the last thirty years, has been called 'English', 'Language' and then, with the arrival of the National Curriculum, 'English' once again. These changes have a significance that is often neglected. The intention of the first change, from 'English' to 'Language', which took place in the 1960s, was twofold. First, it was intended to suggest a truth that was becoming increasingly obvious as society became more and more multiracial: that English was not the only language through which children in the UK expressed their humanity. In that decade, children and teachers in our schools became accustomed to users of many different languages. They struggled to make those children welcome, and to overcome what were seen, insultingly, as their disadvantages. Later, teachers tried to see those children as enrichments to our classrooms. They owned, after all, something very few native English speakers owned, in that they were bi- or even multilingual.

Second, the change to the term 'language' suggested another truth that was becoming increasingly obvious to teachers: that children learned language during their study of other subjects. How can you study Geography or History without studying words? As Simon Rattle was to point out later while deploring the diminished status of the arts in schools, skills used in reading music contribute to skills used in reading literary texts. All teachers have seen children in the nursery tighten their grip on spoken English as they stand over a painting table making pictures together, or as they negotiate roles in making a giant model, or in dancing, or in making music.

But as a profession we were forced to go backwards. The next change – back to the old-fashioned 'English', in the 1980s – signalled the move away from a holistic curriculum, back to a splintered and subject-based one. And back, which was worse, to a curriculum that neglected the bilingualism of many of our children. Under the new dispensation, which we can date from the beginning of the first Thatcher government, if children learned about their language while studying, say, Music, or Geography, it was by-the-way learning that was nowhere near as significant as the learning in their English lessons.

Then, at the decadent fag-end of the last millennium, under the Blair government which had promised so much to teachers, and which has delivered so powerful a kick in the teeth, English lessons gave way to literacy hours. The change to 'literacy' represents a further backward leap towards a mechanization of the teaching of language and children's learning. It takes away elements like unpredictability, surprise and delight, and replaces them with their opposites, so that what happens in a successful literacy hour could have been foretold by the half-alert teacher (indeed a half-alert adult peering in from the street) and has been foretold by many a half-alert inspector. What happens rarely makes the heart (whether the children's or the teacher's) jump.

It is worth noting that the word 'literacy' was formed towards the end of the nineteenth century merely as 'an antithesis to illiteracy' (*Shorter Oxford English Dictionary*). It is a notion developed in reaction to a gross negative. Contrast that dubious pedigree with the heritage of words like 'English', 'language' or 'poetry'.

The place of poetry and other forms of creative writing

In this movement from English, to language, to English again and then to literacy, poetry in particular had a role of fluctuating importance. It was rarely seen as central. But my view of its teaching role (see my list on p.xv) never wavered. If my claims for its powers are justified, the activities in this book are invaluable, necessary even, because they involve children in learning about what constitutes the whole curriculum. What else is there but me and you and all the others, the things we have inherited (nature) and the things we have made, for good or ill? The power of poetry is the power to teach children about the world; to teach, in other words, everything. With the kind of intensive writing we call 'poetry' or 'creative writing' we can teach science, history, geography, personal, social and moral education, art, music and, if pushed, even mathematics. Poetry shows that, despite the grid pressed down by succeeding governments with increasing force on the curriculum, learning really is holistic.

The teacher, poetry (and the teacher poetry is present in the teacher prose, as I will show later) helps us to understand; it comforts us, keeps us going. To put it in other words 'More and more mankind will discover that we have to turn to poetry to interpret life for us, to console us, to sustain us' (Matthew Arnold quoted in Eagleton 1978). How far this is from the mechanical view of language, learning and poetry that we see made evident in the Literacy Strategy, where dead notions like 'concrete poetry' and notions that have never lived, like 'thin poetry', are enshrined and foisted *via* a cynically willing publishing industry on a harassed teaching profession.

Arnold's claims are huge, but they are even more valid today than they were at the end of the nineteenth century. Poetry can help us to put back at the centre of our lives, and the lives of the children we teach, metaphysical truths. All writing that is focused on learning can do this too. These metaphysical truths are truths that the Machine – as R S Thomas (1993) calls the destructive dehumanization that characterizes human life today – has pushed to the edge, and even over the edge. This machine is what has made us think purely in terms of money and profit, and which has made a false god of the market; which has allowed the money-changers into the temple of education; which has taken away 'more than the usual order' and 'more than the usual feeling' (to quote Coleridge, cited in Hourd 1949:174) and replaced both order and feeling with naff little notions like concrete poetry, and thin poetry, and calligrams. 'A poem about fear might be written in shaky letters to represent trembling' the National Literacy Strategy fatuously tells us.

Language, English, literacy and poetry have always (quite rightly) been obsessions for teachers as long as I can remember. We know children have to learn to read and write to take their place in society's work and play. Less certainly, we know too that children are deprived, emotionally and spiritually, if they don't have the sheer pleasure of words sparking along their nervous systems as early in their lives as is possible.

So, why a new book? And why this one? What does this book offer? How does it help us develop ourselves professionally within the fields of literacy, poetry and across the whole curriculum? We need a new book because too many of the books we as teachers are familiar with are mechanical in approach. Their authors have accepted the whole of the new thinking, where everything is seen in terms of cause and effect; where nothing is worth teaching unless it can be measured, and unless it contributes to the effectiveness of the national economy. This means two further things. First, that the books treat children as passive receivers of wisdom; and second, that they treat grammar, punctuation and spelling as priorities rather than servants to content, delight and learning. This book, in contrast, invites educators to treat children as active learners who bring much knowledge to the school – whether in ordinary classtimes, or in the literacy hour – and who bring to school lives full of material that needs to be written about. This book tries to bring children's innate creativity up against the best of current practice in literacy – and attempts to be fair to both.

Second, writers of other books on teaching poetry and literacy (or, more likely, one or other of the two) rarely show appreciation of the fact that poetry is more than something beautiful. It is not an ornament to be displayed or put away at will. It is not a 'pretty' thing with 'the efficacy' (as Elizabeth Bennet puts it in *Pride and Prejudice*) 'of driving away love', or something that we should 'forswear' on growing up 'along with pink ribbons' ('Holy' Hannah More, quoted in Lindop 1981). It is something altogether more central. It is a teacher or, if we prefer, a research tool. It is, whichever model we choose, a way of learning, a way of knowing.

The poems we read to children bring a potent presence into the classroom – that of the poet. I have been most aware of this while working with Shakespeare's works with children (Sedgwick 1999c). For example, I wrote a line from *Antony and Cleopatra* (3:13:20–21) on the board, and we said it a few times, until we had internalized its rhythm and at least the top layer of its meaning: 'He wears the rose / Of youth upon him'. Challenged to pay homage to this line, to imitate it, to use its structure while changing its words, the children wrote: 'He wipes the dust of innocence off his shirt'; 'She dries the wet peachy face of eighteen births off her'; 'She lets out the glow of human sunshine around her'; 'He carries the tattered robe of earth with him'; 'He carries the oak tree of age in his mind'; 'He drags the thorny bush of spite behind him'; 'He wears the weed of weakness about him' and 'He flies the flag of fame in his hand'. In all this I was aware of a ghostly presence; that of Shakespeare and a tiny part of his method. Shakespeare, who lives daily in theatres all over the world as a dramatist, and in studies as a poet, was here alive again as a teacher!

Other writers, like Blake, Thomas Hood, Christopher Smart and Wilfred Owen, have also taught children during my writing of this book. I am embarrassingly aware of the absence of women in that list. This tells us more about the status of women down the ages, and the way society has suppressed their creativity than (I hope!) it tells us about my prejudices. I note that among just over two hundred poets represented in Helen Gardner's almost official *New Oxford Book of English Verse 1250– 1950*, eight are women. The count would probably be more depressing if I were to use the *Golden Treasury*. I wish I could say that the poems of Elizabeth Barrett Browning, Aphra Benn and Alice Meynell opened themselves to children, but I did not think they would.

Yet other writers, still alive, have taught children in a literal way, and later I will suggest ways in which to arrange and gain maximum benefit from a visit to a school by a poet (pp.181–5).

So the poets teach children. Also, poetry teaches children as children write it. It helps them to get the world right, to alleviate the essential dread we all have when we are young of misunderstanding the setting we are in, whether that setting is physical, emotional, spiritual or intellectual. I offer examples of this throughout this book and throughout both my 1997 and 1999c books.

Writing this book has helped me as a teacher to 'develop [myself] professionally within the fields of literacy, poetry and across the whole curriculum' (as the National Literacy Strategy puts it) by widening my visions of what literacy can be; that it might be more than a response to 'illiteracy'. My hope is that it will have a similar effect on my readers, whom I see dimly in the back of my mind as I write, teachers who want to use poetry to get the very best out of their children, and to use children's freshness and enthusiasm to get the very best out of poetry; teachers who are interested in widening their vision to bring into the classroom the creativity I've mentioned – and perhaps even some poets.

The use of structures to help children write

'Art has to be put in prison before it can be set free' noted Leonardo da Vinci somewhere. Goethe said something similar in a poem: 'To attain the good we must confine ourselves / We do the truly good in being limited / And only rules can make us free' (tr. Roeves unpublished). Free verse – where children can write without any sense of structure – actually imprisons them; it is essentially totalitarian, in control. Learning about strict forms sends the writer off on a 'search for words, [a chance to] select, reject, consider, make discoveries' (Byatt 1988).

Looking again at Leonardo's sketchbooks, I think I know something of what he and Goethe meant. He gave himself the task of understanding, for example, the motor muscles of the lips and the mouth (Clayton 1992), or the way a church with its altar at the centre would work (Whiting 1992). The art that came from these speculations has a feel of being produced at top pressure; of exploding from a confined space. With children it is the same. If we ask them, airily, to write about what they can hear, they write in a loose, ineffective way. If, in contrast, we give them a prison, a structure, the writing has a new intensity. I asked the writer of this poem, along with her ten-year-old classmates, to close her eyes and listen for what she could hear in the room, and what it sounded like. I deprived her, briefly, of her sense of sight. Then I asked what she could hear inside her body. I widened the questions to the field outside the window, and to the things she would love to hear, but couldn't.

> I heard the door creaking
> like a haunted house.
>
> a slight whoosh every few seconds
> a slight puff that resembles a horse foot hitting the sand.
>
> I heard a thump like a ten ton dragon hitting the ground and making my body tremble.
> I can hear my eyes swoosh around like rough pebbles being smoothed in the sea.
>
> I can hear the leaves twitching like a cat's whiskers.
> I can hear the north wind trying to make our world into a winter wonderland.

I would like to hear
a swan's song
a deer's voice vibrating
the footsteps of an Irish dancer.
The sound of the sea in a storm.
The sound of lightning.
The splash of professional dancers.

This poem was written during the class's literacy hour (liberally interpreted by me, with permission from the staff) and I think this leads to a further point. We can lighten up a little, given these anxious times, by seeing the literacy hour itself as a structure, as a prison cell that we can use – if we keep our imaginations alive and our spirits intact – to set our spirits and our children free. If we use the strategy to 'encourage, expect and extend' children's thinking (however vague those terms are), it will have served a purpose, as we discover what those 'e' words mean in the practice of our work in the classroom.

Word processing

One of my principles states that **There is more than one way to compose**. A word processor is invaluable for children writing. But despite the computer revolution that has rumbled on over the past twenty years inside and outside schools, children do very little word processing in classrooms. The computer's strength in this area is largely restricted to labels for display and for what are called 'fair copies'. This sells computers and, rather more importantly, children short. It neglects a massive contribution that Information Communication Technology can make to our teaching of English. First, computers take away much of the clerical drudge from writing. Second, computers (and this is far more important) change our way of thinking about what we are writing about. This latter point arises from the fact that using a word processor, I can change the order of these paragraphs within a minute by using cut and paste; on Windows, Control C and Control V. I highlight a passage, press Control C, and the passage is held; I move the cursor, press Control V and that passage is now in its new position. If I press Delete after holding the passage in Control C, it will be in its new position. If I don't, I will have the passage in two positions. I have found that this practice has actually made my way of thinking more flexible. Walking along a street, I can re-order my thoughts for a lecture or an article with this word processing model in mind. Children need opportunities to work with first drafts on computers, so that they can get the benefit that those computers bring of liberating their thinking.

A third use of computers is that they help children to publish their work in the classroom and the school in order to make it more readable. This means that children can make documents that are readable, in the limited, literal sense, for each other to read.

The journey

I am what one of the brother/sisterhood has called a 'jobbing poet'. There are dozens of us, many ex-headteachers (as I am), passing each other on the main roads of Britain; working in a school for a day or two and then moving on. We are free of the 'useless bits of paper' that Causley identified in education in the 1950s (1975:141), and which have spread like leprosy since those relatively innocent days (long-term plans, short-term plans, mid-term plans; special needs assessments; records of support; individual education plans; policy documents; letters from DfEE, OFSTED and anyone, really, who feels like having a pop at my profession).

I have traded in long-term, or chronic, headteacher-stress, for white knuckle, or acute, stress – am I on time? Will this traffic jam ever loosen up? Did they send me directions? I have got a good bargain, though. Travelling poets usually leave school between four and five o'clock and our work at home is writing. We have plenty of time to reflect – in the car, in our studies – on what writing can do. Hence this book. And the great freedom of writing is that you can make the world what you want it to be when you write.

(On the other hand, we don't get to know children so well, except for those children in enlightened schools who book us year after year. One negative result of this is that we rarely get opportunities to help children redraft and edit, and these important activities are not covered sufficiently in this book.)

I mention my travels here for two reasons: first, knowing something about how I work might help the reader to see the children's work printed here in the context of these journeys. And second, a central metaphor is the journey itself: mine in discovering English poetry, which began when I was eleven years old, and mine again in discovering children, with their openness to all experience, especially, as far as I am concerned, language; and the children's journeys – discovering poetry as well, but also themselves and their worlds. Travel with me and the children, and see if Vico's amazing statement – unfashionable as it may be – isn't in fact true: that '… poetic truth is metaphysical truth, and physical truth which is not in conformity to it should be considered false'.

Note

I own up to what will become obvious: a bias towards poetry. This does not matter: all intensive teaching of the writing of poetry will contribute to the quality of children's prose.

Part I

Poetry and science

1 Observing the human body

'an eye for such mysteries'
Thomas Hardy

As I have written in the Introduction, certain statements about children and their writing are so important that, for me, they have the status of **general principles**. I have printed them, in the early stages of my book, in **bold letters**. Later on, I hope that they become implicit in everything that I write, and I drop the bold lettering.

The first principle is this:

Observation

We begin where all studies begin: with **the principle of observation**; with the study of 'this recalcitrant, inescapable "there-ness" of what I call everyday objects' (the artist Frank Auerbach, quoted in Tunnicliffe 1985:8). What I write in the next two or three pages goes for almost every lesson in this book, for almost every stage on my journey. Children need to be encouraged to foster their habit of looking. Herbert Spenser wrote in 1929 'After long ages of blindness [we] are at last seeing that the spontaneous activity of the observing faculties of children has a meaning and a use'. In 1929, 'object lessons' were fashionable, when children drew from observation. An anonymous contemporary account describes how

> … Mr Salter placed at the front of the room on his desk various grasses in a pot, and instructed us to draw them as carefully as we could …

But this (as we can well imagine) did not go very far. And there is very little evidence in educational books since then that children have ever been encouraged to look at anything (as Blake tells us we all should) 'until it hurts'. At the beginning of a new millennium 'The world is [still] troubled / With a lack of looking' (Tardios, quoted in Pirrie 1987). Talking to adults who have returned from a holiday, one finds few that can describe the shapes and colours of buildings that they have seen every day in Blackpool, or on the Cornish coast, or in the centre of Rome or Paris.

All those doors, windows and roofs – different in every part of the world – have gone unseen. Put an adult in the middle of a room where the walls are covered with pictures, and s/he is more than likely (in my experience) to take no notice of them at all.

Children, on the other hand, do look. Babies in prams gaze at leaves moving above them in the breeze, and the sunlight shining through the leaves. I saw a slide of Italian children looking at the underside of a tortoise reflected in a mirror placed under the tortoise, and their gaze was intense. Later, as toddlers, children stare down drain covers. If we are careless in our thinking, or over-careful in our parenting, we see this as an obsession with dirt. It is, in fact, a rampant curiosity. Children gaze at animals, fascinated by the world of creation.

The babies and tortoise image seems to me to sum up one of the strengths of childhood that we as adults, mostly, have lost. Helen Dunmore, the poet and novelist, was quoted by Suzie Mackenzie in the *Guardian* (26 August 1999) as saying that 'when you look at a ten-year-old child "before they have gone through the electric storm of puberty", how savagely observant … they are'. Part of the function of the teaching of poetry writing (indeed, the teaching of all the arts) is to keep that curiosity, that fascinated, even savage, observation alive. That curiosity exists to make us stay men and women 'who notice such things' as tortoise and drain, building and cloud; picture and statue; who have 'an eye for such mysteries' (Hardy 1969:521 'Afterwards').

Concentrated looking, then, is natural to a child, and education, or, at a lower level, schooling, should be focused on helping children to retain that curiosity, and on helping them to develop techniques for intensifying their looking. This is not to say that scientific observation is a simple matter. Even though children experience it as such, it is complex. There are two problems.

First: by observing, we almost always change what we are observing. Here is a simple experiment to show this. Watch a baby closely for a few minutes. Soon your intense look will cause the baby to do something – to smile, or to move towards you or away from you, or to cry, or to ask for food or drink. Your looking at the child has changed that child from someone involved in (literally) God knows what to someone interested in, and suddenly affected by you.

This is, not entirely incidentally, a lesson that OFSTED inspectors could usefully learn. They affect the morale of a school so much that they don't see the school at all, but only the school as altered by them: their unusual clothes, their manners, their questions, their presence in a room, intensively and distressingly imagined even when they are absent. The inspectors I watched, as I worked in a school on my journey around the country, seemed to be completely unaware of the influence they were having. Or perhaps they didn't care. I wrote about them:

> A woman power-dressed in a deep pink suit and clipping high heels appears suddenly in a year six classroom. The teacher is setting the class a task on Victorian England. The inspector's eyes move around the room to watch children as they answer questions. She begins making notes. Then, when the children are writing silently, she asks the teacher something that I can't hear. The

teacher shakes her head: she doesn't know the answer. Both women are slightly bothered about this. But it is the teacher's problem. The inspector can wait, and she does. The teacher stops teaching in the silence while she looks, increasingly worriedly, for a sheet of paper on her desk.

Later in the staffroom, all the teachers' heads turn when anyone enters, even though the OFSTED team has its own space, and won't be coming in. When it is only me, or the headteacher, or the caretaker, their shoulders sag with relief. The caretaker is a puzzled man: his normal easy relationship with the teachers is under strain. Someone says 'They're in bad cop mode today, not so friendly … ' I watch as, just outside the staffroom, a teacher flying from her classroom for cover is caught. The inspector questions her; listens to the answer, and then asks another question without any comment. She does not pretend that this is a conversation among equals …

Sedgwick, 2000c

So, by observing, we change what we see.

Second, no one sees in an unbiased and neutral way. Here is another experiment. With a group of friends, watch a social incident unfold. Try a meeting in a pub, a fight in the street, a reunion between generations. Then compare accounts of that incident. They will, of course, be very different, for the same generic reason that the four gospels are different from each other in their accounts of the ministry of Christ. The act of looking is a selective act, and we select along the lines that our previous experiences and our innate prejudices dictate. One might argue that, because we are involved in such situations, we are bound to disagree about them. But we see even neutral events differently from one another – try storms, sunsets and spring mornings. We are all different. (There is a lesson for those inspectors here, as well.)

But, despite these problems, we still have to look, or we cannot begin to study. We have to examine, and our primary sense is our sense of sight. In looking 'until it hurts', we are doing good science, and we are beginning the business of poetry. 'Darwin', Redgrove (1987) says, 'is a man alert in his world'. In other words, he behaves like a poet as well as a scientist. 'The scientific prose which appears … to be objective has in fact got a very strong feeling tone in it rather like a poem has, in its own way' (Redgrove again). Later in the book, I will show how children observe intangible, numinous things. We are on more certain ground here, though, with our bodies; in particular, to begin with, our hands.

Open the curtains please

Steven was ten when he wrote this poem about observation, and it says a great deal in a few words about this principle. I had read his class Miroslav Holub's poem 'The door' (widely anthologized, most recently in Wilson 1998:2):

Open the curtains please,
get some light in this room.
Get rid of the darkness and have some light.

Let's look at the sun.
Let's look at the roses.
Let's look at the wet grass
with a carpet of dew on it.

Look, just enjoy this moment. It won't,
it won't happen again, I know it won't.
Look, just look through the glass in the window.

See the sky, see other houses.
Look at anything you can.
Just look.
                        (originally published in Morgan 1988)

Another child wrote, while in the grip of Holub's poem:

The Window

Run over to the open window
maybe there will be
a bush
a field of animals
or a secret palace
in the sunshine

Run over to the open window
may be there will be
a cat chasing
a nose sniffing
or a gate
talking in the daylight

Run over to the open window
even if the pine is falling
even if there's a window fighting
even if there's a tree wishing

at least

there will be

a breeze
left in the air
                        Daniel (10)

An infant teacher friend read this poem, and Holub's, to a group of five-year-olds, and then took them on a tour of their JMI school. The words they offered her, and which she wrote down as they walked, show how even the most ordinary of environments repays careful looking:

Open the door.
There are some children
climbing, swinging up ropes,
moving in different ways
through over and round,
hanging upside down.

Open the door.
It's locked.
Could be a monster,
could be a ghost,
a unicorn person,
a wonderland,
a marshmallow man.

Open the door.
A Christmas cupboard,
decorations, light,
red, green, sparkly,
all different colours,
glittery light.
Two fairies are looking for teeth.
When the light's off
it's dark and scary.

Open the door.
There's flowers behind it,
trees, daisies, buttercups, grass.
It's lovely and sunny.
The sky is blue
with fluffy clouds.

Open the door.
A classroom covered with paintings,
marks on the wall
painted all different colours.
A toy looks like the sun.
There's a birthday boy, he's 9,
a puppet all tangled up.
It's Mr Big Ears,
spring on his head,
no hair,
red cheeks,
chubby nose,
smily face,
poppy out eyeballs.
A classroom covered with children

writing, drawing, laughing, smiling,
talking, lots of friends together.
Open the door.
Messy. Junk.
paints, red folders, paper,
jars, lots of flowerpots, Lego,
potatoes, dirt,
clipboards, chess horse, boxes, crayons,
all different stuff.
Gold paper.
More like a junkyard, more like a pigsty.

Five-year-olds' class poem

Poetry and science seem to be odd companions to some teachers who assume that these two methods of thinking, feeling and learning about the world and our relationship to it have nothing to do with each other. To be scientific, for them, is to be coldly rational, unemotional, dry skinned. To be poetic, on the other hand, is to be sweatily obsessed with feelings, and oblivious to the truths that reasoning helps us to understand. This phony opposition involves stereotypes; vague images of cold-eyed scientists in Hollywood films and, in contrast, drunken poets scrabbling about in carrier bags amongst the brown ales and the gin for the next poem that they are going to read.

I have the profound connection between the two disciplines on good authority, both scientific and poetic. The Czech immunologist and poet Miroslav Holub, who wrote many poems that we can use with children, including 'The Door', quoted above, and 'A Boy's Head', said in an interview that his 'intellectual aspiration [is] to bring the hard-centred approach of science into poetic thinking'. Warming to his theme, he continued, '... in science we think in metaphors; when writing poems I do an experiment all the time with a possible "yes" and "no" answer ... '. Ted Hughes (1967) spoke of descriptions in poetry by children: '[They] will be ... scientific in their objectivity and microscopic attentiveness'. Herbert Spenser (1929) wrote that:

> science is itself poetic. The current opinion that science and poetry are opposed is a delusion ... Science opens up realms of poetry where to the unscientific all is a blank ...

One of the most powerful observational activities is to look closely at our own bodies. The children who wrote these next pieces – all seven years old – have been examining their hands, and I have extracted sentences from their writing. I note now that these sentences are composed almost entirely of similes. I suppose that those similes arose from my emphasis on the word 'like': what are your knuckles/fingers/nails like? What do they resemble/remind you of? (For definitions of, and comments on, terms like 'simile', see p.193.)

My palm is like bent sticks. My hand is like a tree with leaves on. In your fingers there are little lines. My hand can bend into a ball …

Sophie

… My hand looks like a skipping rope, or a bamboo stick …

Bradley

My finger looks like a person walking along and like a sign saying stop and go.

David

All you have to do is click your finger and I can walk.

Hasima

My hand is like a cobweb with a spider in.

Kelly

On the side of my hand there is a swirly whirly pattern. My knuckles are like the bony humps that cars go on.

Shaunna

On the palm of my hand is a volcano.
The palm of my hand sometimes I read.

Alice

My hand looks like a bird's feet.

Kelly

Learning from children's writing

I have had more time to examine this work than most teachers usually have. But I am sure that if we could look at children's writing in a more rigorous and respectful way, we would find much to learn from it. In other words, we might find it useful to apply the observation principle, not only to the objects being observed, but also to the children's behaviour as writers. I am going to attempt an examination of that kind here.

First, I note that the children live with different options: 'My hand looks like a skipping rope, or a bamboo stick'. That little word 'or' matters. Children are ready to be provisional. They are happy to consider different versions of the same event. Adults tend to think that only one version can be true, but children, being closer to the clouds of glory that they dragged into the world, know that life (and death) is more complicated than that. Is it a skipping rope, or is it a bamboo stick? 'Let's put both down', a voice in their heads wisely suggests, 'at least for the time being'. If we read, or listen, attentively, Bradley will teach us something about having to be patient; about having to wait between two apparently contradictory truths.

Second, I note the richness of what they write: 'My finger looks like a person walking along and like a sign saying stop and go'. The cobweb and the 'bony humps that cars go on' are neat images. Children surprise us with this richness, as long as we are constantly alert to the possibility of surprise. The skipping rope/bamboo stick line is surprising, and so is 'All you have to do is click your finger and I can walk'. The second of these seems to be influenced by the experience of being a child in a school, at the clipped beck and call of any adult shouting or snapping fingers.

Third, I notice that the writing teaches us something about poetry in general and how children see it. The sentence 'The palm of my hand sometimes I read' is interesting, but I cannot say why is it written in this unusual order. Sometimes children are aware of old poetic traditions, gained, for example from nursery rhymes or hymns, where reversals of the usual order are legitimate, to allow for rhyme, or a requirement of metre. Something of this ancient sense of poetry is contained in another line, not quoted above: 'I fitted it in a poem way' – what did Adam mean? He went on to explain, 'I arranged it, sort of, from the middle ... ' and seemed to be trying to explain why his lines did not go to the right hand side of the page.

The shape of a poem is all part of an ancient definition of poetry that we may as well be aware of in our teaching. Poetry is an art that makes things unfamiliar in various ways:

- it uses lines shorter than the lines of prose;
- it uses strange word orders;
- it uses rhyme;
- it uses metre;
- it strives for comparisons that surprise or even shock us, usually in the form of metaphor or simile.

The last of this list is more useful for us as teachers and young children as writers than the others. Striving 'for comparisons that surprise or even shock us' is more likely to produce a creative buzz or spark than the use of strict rhyme or metre.

The next group of children examined their own feet:

My heel feels smooth as a slide and hard like a brand new wooden spoon.
My big toe reminds me of a tiny football, round and hard. It smells of my
    Dad's old socks.
My little toe reminds me of my puppy because it is small and cute.
It feels hard as a small smooth pebble.
My sole reminds me of a dot to dot picture half finished. It is shaped like an
    upside-down rainbow curved and sleek.
When I feel my ankle it reminds me of the warm cooked bones my mum
    cooks for our dogs. It looks like a twisted bumpy road through a steep
    snowy mountain.

                                                                    Stevie (9)

Smooth soft skin
hard at the end
with curly whirly patterns on top.
Small round bouncy like little marbles with a shiny coating

Krissie (10)

I need hardly say the children had to look with great attention at their feet, think-ing all the while of words that might help them in their writing. Then I encouraged them to think of things that their feet resembled, or looked like. The work 'like', again, is vital here in this sense. It makes them move mentally from the immediate object out into their wide world. It helps the children to make similes.

Then we shared some of the lines the children had thought of. I praised each one, but especially those that had moved away from the status of cliché: I was rela-tively cool with lines about the smell of feet being like the smell of cheese, for exam-ple. They came, even though I was just asking the children to look. When there was an especially original visual line, I asked the child to write it down 'not worry-ing about the spelling just now – get it down – it's too good to lose'. On other occa-sions, I have asked children to feel their feet, and this adds vigour to what they write: 'my heel feels' (one child wrote) 'like a boxing glove'.

Eventually all the children were writing.

Three keywords in this lesson apply to every lesson in this book. They are

- observation,
- simile,
- praise.

Let me sum them up in another way. The more children look, the better. They should keep the words 'like' and 'resemble' in their heads as they look, because this intensifies that looking and that learning. What is this object like? What does it resemble, or remind me of? And when children come up with the goods, as they surely will, let's praise them.

Here are some infants – year one in September – composing a class poem about their knees, as part of a project on the human body. I asked the questions, the chil-dren gave the answers, and the teacher wrote the answers down:

The back of my knee feels soft and smooth like a sponge.
It's like there's fur inside you.
Two hard bits feel like pegs.
My calf feels rough.
It feels like a wriggly muscle.
Like a wibbly wobbly jelly.
It's dribbly, like a ball.

My elbows are round and pointy like round triangles.
They are like red arrows ...

This work depends entirely on sympathetic, pointed questions, with the constant hint in the air that what the children say will be valued.

Looking at eyes

This is an opportunity to test those principles again. The children involved in my next session sat in a circle at desks with paper and pencils in front of them. I asked them to look in each other's eyes carefully. They did this easily and with great attention; and with no embarrassment. They looked in a way that, I suspect, very few adults could do. The will to see, to understand, was greater than their perception of any possibility of embarrassment. In fact, I doubt whether the possibility of embarrassment occurred to them. Then I asked them questions:

What does the middle part look like?

The white part?

The black hole? The eyelashes?

I asked them to keep on looking and thinking, **without putting their hands up, because a child with a hand up is competing, not thinking or looking.** (This has the status of a general principle: a child with a hand in the air is usually – not always – wasting her time. Consider, in this context: a Martian visitor to a school would be very surprised that juvenile humans have to raise a hand and wave it about, saying urgently 'Sir!' or 'Miss!' before being allowed to speak.) After about a minute of intense looking, I asked the children for answers. They came pouring out, and at each one, I asked them to write it down.

And they wrote:

> Billie's eyelashes feel like the spikes of the grass ... when they're closed, Billie's eyes look like a desert. I can see a tree, which is the veins with no leaves on ...
>
> Natalie (8)

> Natalie's eyes look like the white waves in the sea. Natalie's eyelashes feel like delicate birds and they look like the bristles of a tree. Natalie's eyelids look like the sun setting on the tall grass.
>
> Billie (8)

This girl drew a picture to illustrate this: the curve of the top of the eye, like a dome; inside a white space, the lid; and under it, the lashes reaching down, and looking like grass. **The visual image that the girl had made fed into her words, and vice versa.** This is another general principle, and one less understood in our schools than others. Children should be free sometimes to interpret their learning with drawings and writing, not with merely one or the other. Many years ago an inspector, Maurice Rubens, told me that there was 'some fine writing' in the school where I was a headteacher. He waited for this to sink in, and then he said 'There is some fine drawing, too'. Pause. Then: 'Why do you always separate the two?' Ever

1 Eye – children's drawing and writing

since that day, whenever I have had the opportunity, I have encouraged children to draw *and* write when learning about objects in a close observational way. Often, while they are making graphic lines on their writing surface, thinking about their writing strengthens their visual and imaginative grasp on the images they are drawing. All lines are what Paul Klee calls somewhere 'lines into knowledge'.

The blue bit looks like a pond with a tadpole in …

Kayleigh (8)

My partner's white bits look like the shape of the moon. My partner's eyelashes remind me of the stars at night. When my partner shuts her eyes it looks like the sun is setting and the moon is coming up.

Holly (6)

Hayley's eyes in the middle were brown like coconuts.
When she winked they looked like hairs waving in the wind.
A branch covering a flower.

Georgia (6)

Chay's eyes look like a camera.
Chay's eyelashes look like a bird's feather.
Chay's eyelashes are like a flickering devil. …

(Chay was suffering with hayfever during this lesson.)

These reminded me that I had worked with older juniors on eyes once or twice, and I turned up this poem:

Six ways of looking at an eye
Red ivy crawling up a wall,
a black spot in the middle of nowhere.
It's an oval shape like the egg you get for Easter
or a spy looking for dangerous crimes.
Black spider's legs on an end of a leaf.
It's a curl wrapped around nothing.
Pauline (10), from Sedgwick 1989

'Six ways of looking' is a technique for stimulating close observational writing derived by Sandy Brownjohn (1980:49) from Wallace Stevens' poem 'Thirteen ways of looking at a blackbird' (Stevens 1965:34). Brownjohn writes:

How many ways are there of looking at something? … The object … is that the children choose a subject and try to look at it from many different angles … The resulting flexibility of mind, and the ability to see things from different angles, cannot but help their approach to other things besides poetry.

That last sentence is very important for me. A poetic technique once again gives strength and focus to activities that are scientific and artistic in nature. But, even more importantly, both the Stevens poem, and this exercise derived from it, teach children about provisionality; they teach children that there are more ways of seeing something, even something we might consider as simple as a blackbird, that are undreamed of in a philosophy that sees things (blackbirds, dreams, learn-ing, love, hate, marriage) as simple, as unrelated to each other, and to our ways of looking.

This simplistic philosophy does not recognize what I have already suggested on pp.4–5 in Chapter 1: that our ways of looking change what we are looking at. Stevens' poems and this exercise work the other, more honest way.

Kennings

Other children wrote kennings about the eye. They were seven years old:

> a white ping-pong ball with a hole
> a volcano erupting
> a wing of a seagull
> a powerful squinter

A kenning is a poem made up of 'things you might call something'. This is how I put it to children. Kennings are made up of, in longer, adult words, epithets for a chosen subject. In the classroom where the eye example came from (p.12) there was a topic on the human body, and I asked the children to write kennings for, first, the ear:

> sound collector
> music lover
> secret hearer
> rambling radar
> side of head satellite dish
> rumbling recorder
> bang experience

Here are some kennings from the same lesson about other parts of the body:

> *Heart*

> a red kangaroo
> a bumper car
> a wobbly spring
> inaccurate shooter
> a malfunctioned car
> a tied-up rabbit
> a blood bubbler
> red life
> a blood sewer

Nose

a ski slope
a golden pyramid
a yellow trampoline
a drink fizzer
a sing cave
a dirty ditch
a snotty slimer

Joint

a drawbridge
a bone bender
a bony crane
an energy capsule
a power pump

Kennings by older children

A heart kenning

A hard beater
A blood pumper
A body saver
A mayhem maker
A message receiver
A body needer
A squidgy ball
A big red drum
A great red sponge
A death attack
                  Anon (10)

Large intestine kenning

A great food carriage
A squashy slide
A dark pink tunnel
A loop of fat
A mixed-up junction
A spaghetti bolognese
A squidgy slime
A long train going round a corner
... A muddly shoe lace
... A giant runner bean
                  Rachel (10)

Here is a note for the hard-pressed teacher who is worried that the pressures of the National Curriculum are driving poetry out of her classroom: kennings work for any topic. For instance, it is worth beginning a few weeks' work on electricity, or the Vikings, or the water cycle, or whatever is the prescribed learning, by asking the children to write kennings on the subject, and then to do the same when the topic is over. This might provide, among other things, an evaluation of how the work has developed, of how much factual learning has happened.

I'll follow you round your body

This next poem was written while the class concerned was studying the human body. I had read them 'I'll follow you' from A *Midsummer Night's Dream* (Act 3, Scene 1). I have discussed this passage at length in Sedgwick (1999b), and presented there many example of children's writing inspired by it. Children are Puckish, and they emulate that character well. I offer this Puckish piece here because of its scientific resonances:

> I'll follow you
> in mazey guts
> I'll follow you
> in your mouth
> I'll follow you
> in your stomache
> I'll follow you
> where all the
> water is
> I'll follow you
> in your ear where
> I can play the drum
> I'll follow you in your
> bladder where you
> flush me down the loo
> > Anon (7)

The teacher of this child said to me words I often hear. Anon is a child 'who hardly ever does very much in writing … I have never seen her write so much, and so good, too'. **This is a democratic subject: it is not just for God's golden children.** Poetry will serve any writer who has enthusiasm for the language, and all children, at least at first, enjoy playing with words: both the individual sounds of them, and the meanings of them in the contexts of phrase, sentence, paragraph, story, and poem. This exercise has simply re-awakened an enthusiasm for language which (by whoever, and for whatever reason) had been put to sleep. Poetry will serve the writer best who is always enthusiastic, of course; and vice versa; but even a little temporary zest and confidence will lead to something fresh, and may become permanent. This applies whatever the ability of the writer. When children apparently

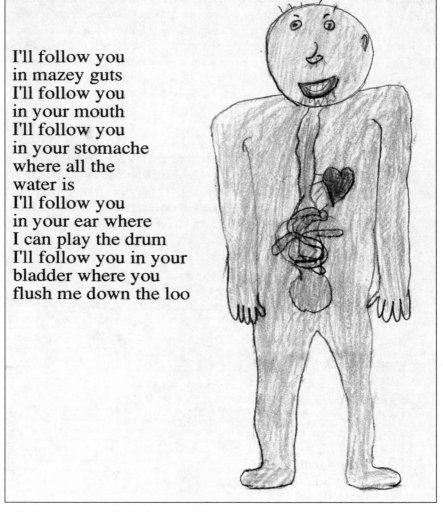

I'll follow you
in mazey guts
I'll follow you
in your mouth
I'll follow you
in your stomache
where all the
water is
I'll follow you
in your ear where
I can play the drum
I'll follow you in your
bladder where you
flush me down the loo

2 I'll follow you – children's drawing and writing

cannot write anything, it is because they have been taught to struggle with words, rather than to play with them.

A further point relevant to this teacher's disrespectful dismissal of a child's abilities is that, other things being equal, the more you expect of young writers, the more they will give you. As a travelling writer-teacher, I can afford to go into any classroom expecting the children to write prose like Jane Austen's and poetry like George Herbert's. This means that they do write well. Teachers who have allowed their expectations to drop find that the children's writing is poor. Their expectations go lower still, in a continuing cycle of negativity that does nothing for child or teacher except produce failure and reduce morale.

I'll follow you
into your ear
and bang away like a wild thing
on your ear drums.
I'll clamber on to your brain
and use it as a bouncy castle
BOUNCE BOUNCE BOUNCE.
I'll creep from there to your eyes
and swing along your lashes
like Superman
and skid down your nose
like it was a ski slope
and land on your tummy.
I'll burrow into your navel
and search around your intestines
and come out from your bum.
I'll play hide and seek
among the toes
on one of your feet
and go to sleep
at the end of your bed.

                    Reggie (11)

2 Fruit, vegetables and other natural things

Fruit and vegetables, with their appeal to the senses of smell, taste and touch as well as sight, always make stimulating contributions to the classroom. First-hand experience is always the best in education. I went to Sainsbury's one evening before visiting this next school to buy a mango, a corn on the cob, courgettes and onions. I also collected some windfalls from our garden: bruised and freckled, most of them, as well as channelled by maggots. In front of the class, I played with the food, slicing, for example, an onion, while the class listened. I asked them what sounds they could hear, and one boy said, with serious intensity while others around him started to giggle, 'At the start the sound is like someone going to the toilet'. I was impressed by the sheer determination of this speaker to get across what he had heard, in spite of what his friends (or his teachers, come to that) might say. Later, he wrote the line in his poem.

> When he was cutting the onion
> it sounded like someone was opening a bag of biscuits.
> It feels like crisp paper
> and smells like pepperoni.
> The colour looks like brown
> and the big bits of onion look like someone's hair.
> The top of it looks like sticks
> and feels like leaves
> The inside looks like white horse skin …
>
> Casey (7)

> It looks like the shape of an igloo
> The cutting sound is like scratching noise.
> At the start the sound is like someone going to the toilet.
> Later it sounds like a fire.
> It looks like the sun and then it looks like the moon.
> It smells like celery.
> Its skin looks like a flower
> The inside of the onion is like an eyeball.
>
> Joseph (7)

Courgette

It looks as green as the grass down below.
It's like silk.
Its pip looks like rain dripping down a window pane
with a swirl like a rushing waterfall.
It smells like an apple that's just been picked.

Rebecca (6)

Seamus Heaney has a marvellous poem which is more than useful in this lesson. You can find 'Blackberry-picking' in at least two places: Heaney (1966:20) and Avery (1994:52). Combined with the first-hand experience – Heaney's words reek of that – this poem will help children to write strongly:

The strawberry I picked
was shaped like a heart.
Its colour was a deep red.

When I bit into it
it melted in my mouth.

When you finish you want more.
You feel like
you're in paradise.

Nikki (8)

The blackberries are filled with a deep purple juice. Each pimple has its own sweetness. The green ones and the red ones will slowly change into huge delicious fruit.

When they are soaking in the cold water, the purple dye floats out of them, leaving pink water.

Some children went on what would have been called, thirty years ago, a 'nature walk' and, after talk about using their eyes, and metaphors and similes, they wrote little poems about berries, stones, sticks and fir cones: perfect material for this kind of looking. We also spent some time talking about the five senses:

I like elderberries.
They look like tiny trees
weighed down by berries.
Each berry looks like a beady eye.
It feels like squeezing a lemon.
The juice looks like wine.
It would taste like a little jar of wine.

Helena (6)

Pine cone

It sounds like a thumping heart.
It looks like a spiky world.
If I tasted it
it would taste like soil and moss.
It is like my head.

Calum (8)

Rose hip

I've always liked rose hips.
It smells of rose smell in a jar.
It feels like stones.
It looks like fire swaying.
If I tasted it, it would taste like the sun, burning hot.
In my body it would be like a muscle, gleaming red.
In the summer it is going to be a rose.

Eleanor (8)

My piece of grass
looks like a green knife.
It feels sticky and smooth.
It smells of fresh trees
swaying in the wind.
It would taste like cooking lima beans.

Claudia (9)

Looking at the weather

The weather was a topic in another classroom, and I read the children King Lear's rage against the storm that begins 'Blow winds, and crack your cheeks' (see my book *Shakespeare and the Young Writer*, 1999c)

Weather,
Get the lightning out of bed,
Send it to work,
Make it crack the earth in half,
Get it to burn everything in its path.

Weather,
Get the rain out of the pub,
Send it to work,
Make it pour,
Drown the earth and all its creatures.

Weather,
Get the snow and ice,
Send them to work,
Make them go,
Get them to freeze everything.

Weather,
Get the thunder to stop eating lunch,
Send him to work,
Make it BOOM, CRASH, CRACK, SHOUT.
Make it deafen
EVERYONE.

Weather,
Get the wind immediately,
Send it to work,
Make it destroy everything

Weather,
I DON'T CARE!

                              Alice (10)

Weather

Snow
freeze us
let us become snowmen.

Wind
hurtle us
strip us to bare bones.

Sun
roast us
frazzle our bones.

Thunder
rumble loud
let the noise shatter our bones.

Lightning
do your worst
hit us over and over until we're ash.

Frost
ice us over
ice us until we are no more.

Rain
melt the ice
turn us into soggy dust
crack the dust into nothing
                                    Daniel (9)

I am not saying that this work (or any of the work in these early chapters) is scientific in every sense. But Shakespeare's words have enabled these writers to observe the weather closely.

Here are examples of extracts from poems written by six-year-olds on a rainy day, this time without the benefit of Shakespeare's words:

The rain
hits the leaf
and squirms off
like a worm
leaving slime
all over the leaf ...

The raindrops are little drums when they hit the ground ...

Every slab of pavement
changes its colour.
The grass is helpless,
it can't run and hide.

A foggy day
I pull the steel trap, step, to find
a cold wispy shudder of mist.
The white flour is cold and lumpy
and not to taste. Pours out before me.
The freeze melts my face
but no water lies at my feet.
It's a white mirror
You cannot touch ...
Your hand disappears in the light dark.
                                    Danielle (9)

The fog is thick as a sheepskin.
Sometimes it looks like smashed glass, like milk spinning ...
                                    Danuella (9)

Again, a child demonstrates an admirable characteristic of young writers that I have mentioned before, an acceptance of provisionality: 'like smashed glass, like milk spinning ... '.

When it comes
cobwebs are just white hair
with hair spray on.
It's a mirror
all smoked up with smoke.
It hits your face
like a spider that has fallen.
You take your glasses off
and everything is blurred.
At night it is like a grey sheet with holes in.

Sarah (9)

Clouds form above my head,
come lower and lower
until they touch
the milk bottle tops …
Tiny clouds gather for meetings …
But some foglings come
and gather trouble …

Sarah (10)

It looks like a golfball crushed

Leon (11)

A supply teacher whom I met by chance on my journey told me that he had asked eleven-year-olds to write about weather 'using a question and answer structure'. This writer uses rhyme and half-rhyme well, until the last line, I felt. But he had certainly made a vivid poem:

Where do you come from, Storm?
From the grim east or the far west?
From high above or down below?

Why, I come from everywhere,
From high and low and over there,
From dark and light,
In day, in night.

So why, so why from up in the sky
Spreading your wrath all over the world,
Flash, bang, boom, swirl?

Why, because I love destruction.
It happens to be my only function,
Throwing my anger down on the world,
Flash, bang, boom, swirl.

So why do you light up the dark evening sky
For people to look upon with wide open eyes?

Why, because it's what I love
To do in the sky above.
It's why I live upon this earth
Though few people know my worth.

Lee (10)

I include this poem because I enjoy it, but also because it is unlike anything else in this book. First, the writer seems to be intent on rhyme, and I usually discourage rhyme for reasons given elsewhere (pp.195–6); here the rhyme gets close to working. Second, the poem has a highly rhetorical character that contrasts with the slightly constrained tone that poems have where the writers are intent on observation, on looking, on learning. Contrast, for example, two lines: the one containing the similes 'like smashed glass, like milk spinning … ' and another that says 'I love destruction. / It happens to be my only function'. The first, the reader might feel, is typical of the work children do with me: tight, observed, obsessed. The second has a tone that no child I have ever taught has felt free to use in my lessons: a little loose, I would say, but taking risks. Here is an eternally important truth: there is room for more kinds of poetry than any one of us has ever dreamt of. For those who are interested in modern poetry, we might say that there is room both for the cautious ironies of Philip Larkin's work, and the for the risk-taking rhetoric of a book like Ted Hughes' *Crow*.

All this writing shows that the numinous is present in everyday things. This is, in my opinion, very necessary knowledge if children are to go through life in an engaged rather than a bored way; if they are to retain some of the sense of wonder with which they are born, and which they must retain if they are to remain philosophers (Gaarder 1995) or poets; if they are to live an examined life; if they are not to live, intellectually and emotionally, from hand to mouth.

As a footnote to that work, here are some six-year-olds thinking about light, and observing in their imaginations a lightbulb, a candle and the sun respectively. They also answered the questions, What are these things for? and What would we do without them?

> The lightbulb is a flashing pear … it is a golden raindrop … It is a white pear in the sun … If we didn't have lightbulbs, we couldn't find a drink and we might die … The candle flame is like an autumn leaf … it helps us to see in the dark, to have a party, to have a date, you put a candle on a café table when you have a date … It is useful for praying in the dark … White drops look like tears … it looks like white paint dripping down … The sun looks like sand at the beach. It is like a hot oven, and it never goes away … If there was no sun, it would be freezing cold. It would be dark, scary and we would be sad … The trees would die …

Some of these comments were spoken by the children, and others were written down by their teachers. I typed others on the class word processor. Among ordinary remarks (not all of which are included here) certain gems emerge: about the date, especially, and the prayer in the dark.

3 Bicycles and other machines

Light, of course, always has possessed a numinous, symbolic significance. 'I am the light of the world' says Jesus, for example, in St John's Gospel, and in common clichés it resonates: 'Let's shed some light upon this' is a significant cliché. Goethe's attributed last words ('Mehr Licht!', More light) give us all pause. What, though, about the numinous in something ordinary? What, for example, about bicycles? What follows are notes I made after an exciting session with children and bicycles in a lovely school called Tacolneston, Norfolk.

I didn't begin with the bicycles. They were there, in the classroom, one at each end, among the displays of paintings and the bookshelves. I'd upended them, or at least two girls on work experience from the local high school had upended them. This made them look unfamiliar. This is important when you want to draw something, or write about it. How you see a sink, or a chair, or a table – or a bike – every day will not help you very much to make your drawing, or your poem, or your description. Deep down you think, I've seen this, I know what it's like, it's like this, and you reproduce the familiar image as you familiarly see it.

This is especially true of children and bicycles, because most children ride them easily, and often see their friends riding them. This causes them to draw what they expect to see, not what they actually see. Of course, they don't draw accurately; they draw, instead, a casually made symbol of what they know about, of what they are familiar with. They get it, not so much wrong, as bland. When you draw the familiar as it is familiarly seen, you are not truly engaged with it. The large sweep of the thing – two wheels, handlebars – is all right, both in the sense of accuracy and in the sense of engagement, but the details (and, notoriously, the god is in the details) are missing, or casually sketched, rather than examined till it hurts, and then striven over. The chain will be muddled in vaguely, and so will other crucial elements, like the brakes, the brake handles and the chain wheels.

But turn the bicycle upside down and the very strangeness of the altered image makes you look at it freshly. You have less excuse for casually, or even carelessly, putting the expected image on the paper.

Anyway, I began, not with the subject, bicycles, but with the media, with the paper and pencils. I gave all the children – aged seven years to eleven – a scrap of paper and asked them to cover it 'with as many different pencil marks as they could think of'.

3 Children and bikes (1)

4 Children and bikes (2)

5 Child's scribbles

Then I asked them to draw part of one of the bicycles. But I gave them four rules. They are, for me, general principles for all drawing:

- **No erasers.** There are three reasons for this. First, erasers waste time. I have watched many children over the years worrying at a sentence or a sketch with an eraser, rather than with their imagination, thus using up time when they could be learning. Second, they encourage children to think in terms of a photographic image of perfect accuracy, rather than an image that engages the viewer. Third, they often rub out wrong lines that are interesting. I show children Alberto Giacometti's drawings, which are notable for the multiplicity of their lines.
- **Do the drawing close up.** This prevents the children making drawings that are so small that their meanings are obscured. It is a better way of putting it than 'Do it big' because it enhances the quality of the looking.
- **Use your pencil in all the different ways you have used it on those scraps of paper.** This empowers the drawings by giving them variety and depth. It surprises the children when you first suggest it, but it guarantees a sudden improvement in all their drawing. In a school that uses this technique as a matter of course at the beginnings of all the school years, the children draw more effectively than in other schools.
- **Look, look and keep on looking.** When they are young children need to be taught that one look at what they are drawing is not enough. They need to keep checking, to keep re-establishing their relationship with their subject.

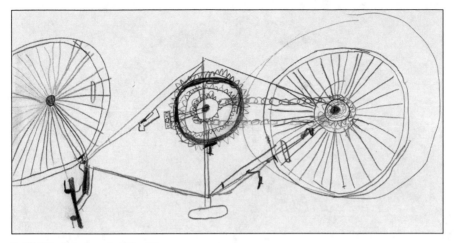

6 Child's drawing of a bike (1)

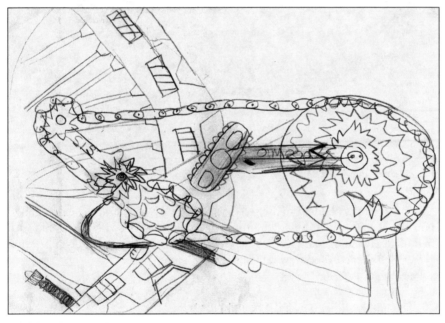

7 Child's drawing of a bike (2)

Here are some of the children's drawings. These drawings, and the ensuing conversations and writing, taught me yet again an old truth, put succinctly here:

> 'Children who learn to look, learn to question, to discover, to understand …
> Looking absorbs, engages, calms and sensitizes the learner … Art is a way of
> looking, seeing, questioning and discovering … '
>
> Newland and Rubens 1984

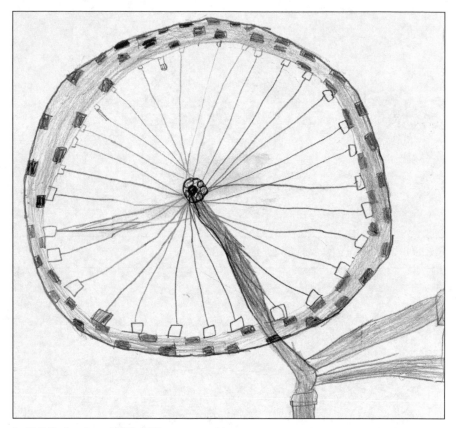

8 Child's drawing of a bike (3)

I also asked the children to listen to the bicycle. We all sat on the carpet, and I spun the wheels, while the children sat with their eyes closed and covered with their hands, listening to the ticking noise. I asked them what it sounded like, what it reminded them of, and we wrote down their words.

They began to write:

> The brakes slither out of the handles like snakes.
> The cogs for the chain
> are waves at a standstill.
> The spokes are jail bars in a cold dark cell.
> The wheel turns into a mirror unexpectedly.
> The frame reminds me of Snoopy with a pedal eye.
> The bike is a muddle of letters.
> O is the wheel
> C is the handle.
> P is the back part of the frame.

Q is the pedal
linked on to a cog.
L are brakes.
U is the chain.
D is the wire crossing.

Ellie (11)

This writer showed extraordinary vividness in her images. Note especially the spinning wheel as a mirror, and the brakes 'slithering out of the handles like snakes'.
The comparison of parts of the bicycle with letters of the alphabet shows another
skill that writers need to develop – a playfulness. This writing is full of both metaphor (note especially 'the cogs of the chain / are waves at a standstill') and simile.

The reflectors spin and whirl
while the spokes disappear
into a new dimension.
The chain sounds like a train
clacking over a track.
The frame is keeping the gears together.
The gears are like
sets of eyes
watching where I ride.
As I change gear
it moves around and around.
A new ride is coming
on each gear.
The chain sounds like
the rain stick in music.
Then suddenly
I hit the kerb.
My bike trips suddenly
My helmet took the fall …
My arm is in a cast
for three weeks.
The spokes of my bike shimmer in the sunlight.
My bike makes me free
in a world of freedom.

Danielle (11)

The rain stick reference stemmed from the fact that there was one of these musical
instruments in the classroom, and we had played with it; then I had read the
children Seamus Heaney's poem 'The Rain Stick', from his book *The Spirit Level*
(Faber and Faber 1996), and played a recording of the poet reading the poem
himself. Classrooms where interesting, strange, surprising objects are on display are
classrooms where lines like this get written. 'The spokes disappear / into a new

dimension' is a daringly original idea. This writer had had an accident on her bicycle, and her arm was still bound up. This lesson gave her the opportunity to bring the story of her accident into the lesson.

> When the pedal goes down it looks like a chequered flag starting a car race.
> The reflector slithers through the spokes.
> The chain is like a conveyer belt moving fast fast fast.
> The sound is like a clock ticking and then speeding up.
> The spokes look like they're going down a whirlpool and coming back out.
> The cogs look like the mouth of a dragon eating its chain.
>
> Matthew (9)

> The bike looks like
> a pair of
> glasses on the wonk.
> The top of the pedal looks like
> a doormat
> that has had a lot
> of muddy shoes wiped on it.
> The spokes make me think
> of when I'm roller skating.
> The orange reflectors
> are the colour
> of my mum's orange jelly.
> The noise of the chain
> is like a rattlesnake
> also
> the noise of chain is like a bell.
> When the wheel is going fast
> if you lightly
> put your hand on the wheel
> you see muck or sand or dirt
> popping up and down.

The next writer gave his poem an appropriate title: 'Objects Connected':

> A large object,
> Connected by a chain,
> Turns to a small object,
> Connected by a chain,
> Small object turns a wheel,
> Connected by a chain,
> Large object turned by a pedal,
> That's connected to the large object,
> Connected by a chain,

To the small object,
Turning the axle,
Connected to the spokes,
Turning the wheel
Makes the bike go faster
Connected to the ground.

Giuliano (10)

Here again the drawing and the poem inform each other. The writer's use of the repeated word 'connected' has been encouraged by the experience of making the line on the picture, and vice versa.

Bits of a bike

The wheel is like a life cycle
going round and round again.

The reflector is like a burning fire
flaming in the night.

The wheel is like a wave
rolling on the sand
on a summer's morning.

The wheel sounds like rain
falling on to the pavement ...

The spokes look like they disappear then reappear like a ghost.

The pedal is a butterfly
spinning round and round.

Lauren (11)

A note about the broader curriculum

In these days when we have to justify every minute a child spends in a classroom, we should ask: What are the children learning as they study the bicycles with their ears, eyes and hands? We can make six strong answers to this question.

First, they are learning mathematics as they look at geometric shapes, especially triangles and circles, and as they count spokes in order to draw them accurately. Second, they are learning science: physics of course, such as how chains and brakes work in general; and they are learning technology, the application of that science for bicycles in particular. Third, they are learning something about their bicycles as a means of transport, and therefore it is not far-fetched to suggest that this work contributes to their safety on the road. Fourth, they are learning about language, and the subtleties of it when it is required to describe something with accuracy. Fifth, they are learning about poetry, and the use of similes and metaphors and other figures of speech; about the little-known fact that poetry is about the workings of bits and pieces of our lives, as much as daffodils and clouds, and how language can be beautiful even when the subject matter is as down-to-earth as their bicycle. And sixth, they are learning about art and its ability to tell us the truth about things; that every line is a line into knowledge. They are learning, too, that art can be aesthetically pleasing and vigorous when it is not concerned with obviously lovely things like flowers and clouds; that what Rupert Brooke, in his poem 'The Great Lover' (Brooke 1932:134), called 'the keen / Unpassioned beauty of a great machine' has its charms, too.

Once, I did something similar with my car engine. It was still at first, then I turned it on. It excited this writer:

> An elephant's trunk withdraws from an ice bucket.
> The elephant is very gritty.
> Four grass snakes crawl into a cardboard box.
> When he revs the car up, the snakes nearly knock the box over.
> When the engine was turned on, the snakes were frightened.
> They were shaking.
> There was a dead snake at the back.
> His head had been burnt off.
>
> Anon (11)

The ferry on the Broads

Sometimes, teachers and children are lucky enough to see and hear a machine that is out of the common experience of most of us. One day in the summer of 1999, on my travels as a jobbing poet, I noted that there was a shorter route to the little school that had booked me in for a day than the way I had planned. The village is on the Norfolk Broads, and I drove confidently towards it, cutting off a huge triangle with Norwich at one corner and the Norwich–Yarmouth A47 by-pass at one side – and found myself facing a ferry.

The great clanking thing had space on it for three cars, and I had enough money in my pocket – just over two pounds – to pay the ferryman, and sufficient time to not be late. The mechanics, the noisy, oily facts of the matter, chains, steering wheels and clanking ramps – competed in my mind with the symbolism. Where do ferrymen take us, traditionally? I thought of the ferryman in Greek mythology, carrying the dead across the River Styx into Hades.

An hour later, in the school, I asked the children to describe their ferry, pointing out first that it was an unusual possession, and that the friends I had met on my travels in Stevenage, Ipswich, Bishop's Stortford, Durham and other places would be surprised – and impressed – to experience one. I told them about the ferry in Cornwall that I knew – bigger than theirs, but less impressive in some ways, because, I think, of their ferry's intimacy. I talked about my experience that morning – about the panic, about driving on to what I thought looked like a steel road; about how much care I took. I talked about the chains I could see, about how I kept testing that my handbrake was on, because of the illusion that the car, not the ferry, was moving.

I said that in their writing the word 'like' would be useful, in its simile-introducing mode, and that I wanted to see some careful descriptions of the sounds the ferry made as it crossed the little river, and also of effects the ferry made on the water. What did it make the water look like, for example? What did the chain resemble, or remind them of? The wheels, the cogs?

For once the children had ready access to word-processing facilities, and to the expertise of a teacher. Also there was a parent who could type properly (unlike me, who types with two fingers), and when the children tired of the keyboard, she took over. The children watched their poems grow on the screens in front of them. This flexibility in the use of word processors seems to me to be as important as it is rare. Often I see impressive computer suites in schools, but they rarely seem to be used to compose poems, stories or reports. In other words, one of their primary functions, word processing, is almost completely neglected. Ideally, each classroom should have three or four computers available when the children are writing so that they have some experience in composing with them. As I said in the Introduction, the facility that these machines have to change the order of words, sentences and stanzas at the touch of a couple of keys actually makes thinking more flexible. Pens and pencils have a more tactile feel, and it would be sad if the next generation forgot the pleasure of using them. But computers have a pedagogic function in writing, and we sell our children short by not giving them access to them.

We printed their poems in little editions of three: one for the writer, one for the publisher, and one for the visitor, me.

The ferry is like a plank of wood floating in the sea.
I hear the chains. They sound like click click or ch ch ch.
I feel calm not scared.
I always know everyone enjoys the ferry from the smile when they come off.

The river jumps on to the ferry.
The person on the ferry looks out for boats.
It moves very slowly.
It makes the river part into small waves.

The chains move around a wheel
and pull the ferry from one side to another.
In summer huge queues come.
In winter there are no cars.

You can't swim in the river
or you will drown.

                    Sarah (8)

The chains creak the cogs,
moan,
the noise is like a car starting.
The water crashes on the hull.

It moves slowly but I don't mind.
The cabin is very small but the driver can fit in.
Levers buttons and cogs alike
are all inside the cabin.
The chains are creaky moving like an old granny getting up.
Two motors work their hardest trying to get the old chug a bug moving.
They always manage in the end …

Stuart (9)

… The water has circles in it that grow bigger and bigger when you throw a
  stick into it.
In the old days 6 men pulled the chains across the river
but now they have electricity …

Sarah (10)

When you look down from your car you can see the chains.
The chains make a creaky sound.
They remind me of the sounds in our diesel minibus.
The cabin is small but the driver manages.
Once the driver short-changed my Nanny …
Sometimes there are big queues. In the time you could run into the pub and
  get a drink …
There are little splashes of water where the ferry had been …

Anon (9)

Notice here the children's casual observation: 'I always know everyone enjoys the
ferry from the smile when they come off'; 'It makes the river part into small waves.
There are little splashes of water where the ferry had been … '

4   Cats and other animals

'If at night your eye is placed between the light and the eye of a cat, it will see the eye look like fire'

Leonardo da Vinci

'He moves slowly and softly/a little bit at a time'

Anon (5)

For some reason, cats and poetry seem to be related. Look at this wonderful extract from a longer poem by Christopher Smart. It can be found in many anthologies, including *The Rattle Bag* (Seamus Heaney and Ted Hughes 1982) and my own *Jenny Kissed Me* (2000d):

> For I will consider my Cat Jeoffry.
> For he is the servant of the Living God, duly and daily serving him.
> For at the first glance of the glory of God in the East he worships in his way.
> For this is done by wreathing his body seven times round with elegant
>   quickness.
> For then he leaps up to catch the musk, which is the blessing of God upon
>   his prayer.
> For he rolls upon prank to work it in.
> For having done duty and received blessing he begins to consider himself.
> For this he performs in ten degrees.
> For first he looks upon his forepaws to see if they are clean.
> For secondly he kicks away behind to clear away there.
> For thirdly he works it upon stretch with the forepaws extended.
> For fourthly he sharpens his paws by wood.
> For fifthly he washes himself.
> For sixthly he rolls upon wash.
> For seventhly he fleas himself ...
> For eighthly he rubs himself against a post.
> For ninthly he looks up for his instructions.
> For tenthly he goes in quest of food ...

I read this poem to a class, and asked them to choose someone – animal, human – that they were fond of, and to write a poem for them in this style:

> For I will consider my cat Jim.
> First he pounces on my bed
> with his almighty legs.
>
> Second, he will curl up like
> a statue of gold.
>
> Third, he will stretch his claws
> and paws to wake him.
>
> Fourth, he will go hunting
> with his bulging eyes
> covering every movement in the grass.
>
> Fifth, he will catch his prey
> and carefully eat
> the flesh of this wild animal.
>
> Sixth, he will jump and play
> and when he is tired
> he will growl and walk away.
>
> Seventh he will run around
> your ankles with his nose
> sniffling your leg.
>
> Eighth, he will go searching
> for a lady cat
> and when he meets one
> he will bush his tail
> and walk towards her.
>
> Ninth, he will guzzle down his bedtime milk.
>
> Tenth, he will pounce on my bed
> with his almighty legs.
>
> Tom (11)

> For I will consider my auntie's horse Trigsy.
> For first he'll rub upon my shoulder to make his neck clean.
> For second he'll give me a big morning hug by making me put my arms
>   around his dusty neck.
> For third he'll be so clean that his fur feels as silky as snow.
> For fourth he gets ready for his long distance morning ride.
> For fifth I get his hacking stuff off and put it neatly away.

For sixth he eats his breakfast while Sheba and Abby the dogs try to get at
    the carrots.
For seventh he'll be given a few Polos for being good.
For eighth he'll follow me to the old creaky gate.
For ninth I release his collar, the brightest in the world.
For tenth he'll be set free for the summer afternoon.

Chloe (9)

This writer had spelling problems. She had written, among other things, 'thirst' for
'first', 'fear' for 'fur', 'stick' for 'stretch', 'checkly' for 'creaky'; and even 'are' for 'I'. The
word 'dyslexic' hovered ominously over her. She wore coloured glasses, which, it was
believed, clarified the letters in front of her, taking away their haziness, and putting
them in focus. And yet, despite these difficulties, she can write 'he'll be set free', playing dramatically with a different tense; she can convey the vivid sense of what it is
like to be in a stables. Above all, she can celebrate her relationship with a horse.

Finally, here is an unusual animal observed with great delicacy:

For I will consider the mud-brown spider in my room.
For firstly he webs his silk web with style.
For secondly he bungee-jumps off the roof
with his silk web, slowly, with little stops.
For thirdly he prowls up the wall like
The Queen of Sheba,
For fourthly he devours his prey with pride.
For fifthly he runs as fast as lightning
so that no predator can catch him.
For sixthly he catches anything that goes in his web.
For seventhly he can last for ages without any food.
For eighthly he hides from humans in books.
For ninthly he scares away unwanted insects
For tenthly he waits for his food to die before he eats it.

'For I will consider my Uncle Graham': for examples of this form using people, see
Chapter 5.

That is one way of writing about a cat: using a structure that Christopher Smart
has already thought of. Another way is to go back to the first principle, **observation**.

Leonardo wrote about his observations of a cat: 'If at night your eye is placed
between the light and the eye of a cat, it will see the eye look like fire'. It is in this
spirit that this child writes:

The cat's eyes are olive green, the shape is like a kiwi fruit. The cat walks
slowly like an Indian searching for food. It strides like it was the most important person in the world. It's curled up like an old football with a dangly bit.
The tongue curls up like a ball.

Anon (10)

Also children can surprise us: 'The tongue drinks up all the milk, like a racing driver, lap after lap after lap'. These last two examples come from *Art Across the Curriculum* (Sedgwick and Sedgwick 1996).

Infants writing about cats

Can infants write? Where you stand on that question says much about your view of what children are. Do you believe that five-year-olds cannot write until they have had certain skills instilled into them? If so, you have a view of children as weak, non-autonomous individuals, and, having that view, you will work in classrooms in ways that establish control over them. If, on the other hand, you believe that children exhibit early signs of writing when they are as young as three years old, in their scribblings on walls and pieces of paper, you have a different view of children as individuals making their mark and asserting their autonomy in the world. 'Once I saw writing / But now I see words' wrote one seven-year-old, expressing something of this view of the development of writing and reading.

Children, I believe, are writers, and if I work in a classroom where they are routinely treated as such, they write. If, on the other hand, I work in a classroom where they see themselves, because of what the teachers have told them, as non-writers, or pre-writers, they do not write. Later, if they have to have every spelling checked before they copy a word into their notebooks, they are being controlled, while writing should be an opportunity for freedom.

Labelling

These drawings show one way of treating very young infants as writers. The children draw first, and are then encouraged to write labels for their drawings, to tell us what everything is. At first they will write single words, but then they can be gently encouraged to add adjectives and verbs. They can also be encouraged to write speech bubbles for their drawings 'like in comics'. All this is a very unthreatening way of giving children the early glimpses of what power over words can do. It is in direct opposition to methods of teaching writing that merely enable us as teachers to establish our control over them: the vocabulary book, the word queue, the view of writing that sees it as being synonymous with correct spelling and grammar.

Children who are treated as autonomous soon grow into powerful writers, and use metaphor and simile vividly:

> The ears are spiky triangles. The eyes are the top of the point on a pen. The whiskers are plastic strips. The nose is a swing. The tongue is sgwisey [?squidgy]. The collar is a medal. The fur is cotton wool. The tail is a rope.
>
> James (6)

> His eyes look like he is saying I want more milk. His fur is like an arrow. His tail looks like an ice cream.

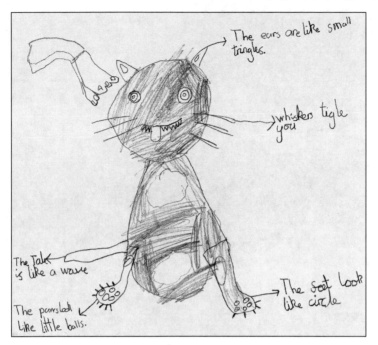

The ears are like small tringles.

whiskers tigle you

The Tale is like a wave

The paws look Like little balls.

The seet look like circle

9 Child's drawing of a cat (1)

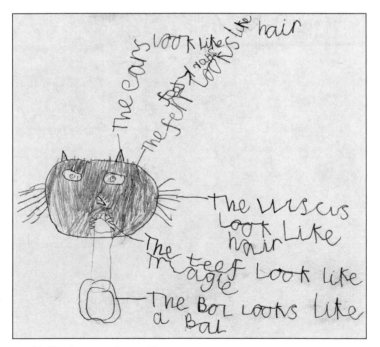

The ears look like hair

The feet looks like

The urscus look Like hair Like

The teef Look like triagle

The Boi looks Like a Bal

10 Child's drawing of a cat (2)

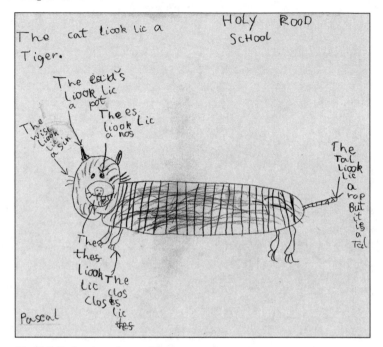

The cat liook lic a Tiger.

HOLY ROOD SCHooL

The eati's liook lic a pot

The es, liook lic a nos

The wisc liook lic a sin

The Tal liook lic a rop But it is a Tal

Thee thes liook lic Clos clos es lic tes

Pascal

11 Child's drawing of a cat (3)

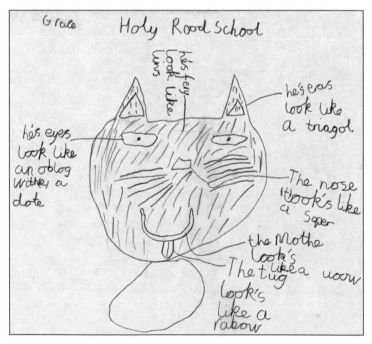

Grace   Holy Rood School

he's fey look like wins

he's eras look like a triagol

he's eyes look like an oblog witheu a dote

The nose llook's like a sqoer

the Mothe look's like a uoow

The tug look's like a rabow

12 Child's drawing of a cat (4)

Inside the little prison cell of the haiku, one child wrote about a cat:

> Cat with angry look
> with his back arching like a
> rainbow without colours
>
> > Caroline (9)

Tyger! Tyger!: a challenge to aspire

> Tyger! Tyger! burning bright
> In the forests of the night,
> What immortal hand or eye
> Could frame thy fearful symmetry?
>
> In what distant deeps or skies
> Burnt the fire of thine eyes?
> On what wings dare he aspire?
> What the hand dare seize the fire?
>
> And what shoulder, and what art,
> Could twist the sinews of thy heart?
> And when thy heart began to beat,
> What dread hand? and what dread feet?
>
> What the hammer? what the chain?
> In what furnace was thy brain?
> What the anvil? what dread grasp
> Dare its deadly terrors clasp?
>
> When the stars threw down their spears,
> And water'd heaven with their tears,
> Did he smile his work to see?
> Did he who made the Lamb make thee?
>
> Tyger! Tyger! burning bright
> In the forests of the night
> What immortal hand or eye
> Dare frame thy fearful symmetry?

This is the most difficult lesson in this book. We might see it as an advanced lesson, and it works best under the following conditions:

- You are interested in poetry or, preferably, passionate about it.
- The writers know you well and your standards and expectations.
- The writers have become familiar with many poems. This means not just poems written for children, but poems from the mainstream of English poetry.

- The class is a stable one, without children who, for whatever institutional reason, lack motivation when challenged with high order work, and who therefore may disrupt the lesson.

Read the children this famous poem. It is, or should be, part of what Philip Larkin called the 'myth kitty' of every educated Briton. It sums up what most of us think a poem is: lucid in places, obscure in others; metrically as regular, almost, as a hymn; rhyming consistently in couplets; packed densely with imagery; rhetorically powerful. Practice it first at home, however well you think you know it. Note the following:

- It begins as it ends, but with one significant change. Ask the children to listen for that change.
- It is almost entirely made of questions.
- The fifth stanza is different in tone from the others. It is also, as far as I am concerned, very difficult. Acknowledge your difficulties with the poem, to legitimize the children's. Note these comments on this stanza by a secondary pupil, Michelle, quoted in Benton *et al* (1988): 'The fifth stanza appealed to me 'cos it ... reminded me of a falling star or a shooting star, and then exploding into a thousand pieces ... like which was heaven crying ... and it was sort of like a rocket on Guy Fawkes' day, exploding in the sky ... '

One way of reading this poem is to begin very quietly, even in a whisper, and grow in a crescendo till you reach 'What the hammer, what the chain', and go down in a diminuendo, until you are whispering the last stanza. You could reverse this procedure, starting loud, getting quiet in the middle, then growing in another crescendo. Then get the children to say the poem line by line after you in the same way that you say it. Play with the poem, missing out words and making them say them. Explain words like 'immortal', 'aspire' and 'sinews'. Ask questions, such as:

> Why is the night a forest?

> Can you list the tools used to make the tyger, and describe them?

> What does 'When the stars threw down their spears, / And watered heaven with their tears' mean'? Emphasize that there is not necessarily a correct answer here.

> Who is this immortal one who made the tyger?

> Why is the poem made up of questions?

Ask the children to choose an animal they could address in such a way, and to write a poem. I might as well say here that I disallowed rhyme:

Dragon, dragon, with your heart so cold
Why do you breathe your fire?
Why do you live in the darkness of your lair?
How do you pass the boring hours of every day, every month, every year?
Dragon, dragon, with your angry soul
Do you like the darkness?
Do you hate it?
Why do you stomp around like you're in a mood,
Dragon, dragon, the fearless one.

Leo (11)

Eagle eagle flying high
Why do you attack little animals?
What wonderful colours you have got.
How do you fly so high?
Do you fly like a swooping jet?
Do you know your yellow beak is as sharp as a nail?
Is it true that your eyes can see for miles?
What a wonderful tail you have got.
Are you the fastest flier or the fastest catcher?
Eagle eagle flying high
Eagle eagle flying high

Anon (9)

Dolphin dolphin
Where do you live?
What is your name?
How do you jump the dark, dark sea?
Dolphin dolphin.

Anon (9)

Oh rabbit rabbit
dark as night
Who gave you power to your eyes?
That gleam so bright?
Who gave you your wonderful black fur?
Where did you learn
to run as fast as a hare?
What memories do you have in your furry head?

Rabbit rabbit
who gave you your gleaming eyes
And why do you run away from me?

Anon (9)

Talk about tools

I did the exercise again, emphasizing the tools that Blake mentions – 'hammer', 'chain', 'furnace', 'anvil':

> Hamster, hamster why are you so small?
> Who chiselled that lovely face of yours?
> Who has sewn that delicate fur all over your body?
>
> Hamster, hamster, how do you stuff your cheeks with that food?
> Who stuck your tiny teeth in your mouth?
> How did they do it to you tiny thing?
> Who made those beady eyes so small and black?
> How does your heart beat so tiny and red?
> Why don't your eyes burn very bright?
>
> Anon (11)

That last line represents delightful unsentimental observation. It must take an effort of the spirit and of the imagination to see the eyes of a creature you love as dim. We see what we can see often enough if we are attentive and vigilant: that children get beyond sentimentality because they are, above all, honest.

These were only partially successful. But the children asked some eternal human questions, about, for example, why animals run from man 'when all I would do' (as Yeats puts it) 'is to scratch your head / and let you go' ('To a squirrel at Kyl-na-no' in *Collected Poems* 1983:155). I tried the idea again, emphasizing grander animals only, and the tools that might have been used to make them. Here are some quotations from the poems, and two complete poems. All these children are ten years old:

> Shark, shark …
> in the bright wave of moonlight …
> Could an immortal crush thy solid bones … ?
> Was it a razor, was it a blade that was used
> to shape thy menacing teeth?
>
> Sae Hoon

> Giraffe …
> who ironed on the spots and scorched your skin?
> How did those jumpleads
> stretch your neck?
>
> Cleo

> What needles sewed the silk to the dolphin?
>
> Danielle

Minotaur ...
who made your horns of infinite power? ...
Who made your muscles
of indestructible strength?

                    Shinwoo

Elephant ...
who was big enough
to make thy hulking shoulders?

                    Jane

Phoenix, phoenix of the sun
Where were you made?
How were you done?
Were you made of silk and pain
Or were you made
Of hard, malignant magic?

Phoenix, phoenix of the sun
Where were you made?
How were you done?
Was your heart shaped by a flame,
Your lungs by sandpaper,
Beak by leather, therefore opaque?

Phoenix, phoenix of the sun
Where were you made?
How were you done
Gliding through the African plains
Guided by the light of Father Sun.

Phoenix, phoenix of the sun
Where were you made,
How were you done?
Your scorched pearly eyes
Reconstructing a figure of the sun,
Recording every movement of it.

                    Nicholas

Seal, seal, swimming gracefully,
What are you from?
From silk for my coat
and marbles for my eyes,
string for my whiskers
and a shiny black button
for my nose.

Seal, seal, swimming gracefully,
Where were you made?
I was made in a glittery ocean
full of tropical fish.

Seal, seal, swimming gracefully,
I was made by the greatest, kindest person.

Natasha

I have had one problem with this lesson. One boy wrote 'Crab, crab, why do you pinch so much' and stopped, put down his pen, and scowled for the rest of the period. I praised his line, and tried to extort more from him with kindness and finally a loss of patience, the expression of which I tried, successfully I hope, to suppress. His teacher told me that 'everything he does has to be perfect or he gives up'. Who has taught him this? Whoever it was has done him no favours, because to write in this way entails risk-taking. It involves getting something down quickly in order to play with it, to work on it. Even if the first few sentences end up being struck out, they will have enabled thought on what will eventually remain. The boy must have felt that I was impatient with him, and on the upper level I was. But really my impatience was with the misguided adults who had mistaught him, suggesting that there is somewhere a perfect object, and that in all his writing, he had to aspire to it. That is as uneducational a notion as is possible.

Another way of getting children writing about animals with freshness is to read them Ted Hughes' poem 'Hawk Roosting' (Hughes 1960:26) This is a monologue, redolent of power and violence, spoken by a hawk at the top of a wood. It attracts children partly because of those very qualities, but also the clarity and the vigour of the language are far from lost on them. I played with the poem. I spoke it twice, the second time explaining some difficult terms. I played Ted Hughes' own recording of it (1977), and asked the children to say it after me line by line. I also read the children Philip Larkin's poem 'Midwinter Waking' (Larkin 1988) which is about a mole or a badger waking too early from hibernation. Finally I asked these children to write monologues for animals themselves:

Hunting Wolf

I stalk the grassy landscape at night
sniffing for the faintest touch of smell
in the fields and farms.
I stare into the black night
waiting for a tiny hint of movement.
Then it comes at me.
A short sharp flash of colour speeds over the empty cornfield
and whips past me like lightning on the ground.
I spin around
and bound after it.

I strain every muscle
just to reach it.
I close in on it.
…
I slash my jaws at the hare
making great wounds in its side.
My jaws clamp together tight.
I stride towards a rock
and climb on it.
I stand up tall and straight
legs pulled up tight and strong.
I raise my head upwards
and howl to the great, white, round moon.

Sally (9)

Fieldmouse

I run rapidly seeing
leaves brushing the ground.
I run through the sugar beet.
I smell the warm herby air.
I see the scattering
leaves flow over me.
I hide under this tree.
The bark is rotten, woodlice in a
line weaving from side to side …

Jesse (10)

Fieldmouse running

I
scamper over
moss and stones
as I gather
together food.
I scurry
in sunlight between
the tall thin
stalks of
corn, it's
like I'm hunting
in a very
vast jungle.
Scampering feet go
past so I
climb to the top

of a tall
thin stick of
swaying corn.
I go scutter
run, scutter, run
scutter, run
until I
find a puddle
to drink from.
          Helena (10)

As the harvest corn mingles with the rich red poppies
the seeds, like droplets fall from the sky as I scamper over the
massy rocks embedded in the stony soil.

An old fallen oak tree lies in my path.
The damp leaves sway in the air as the spiders crawl over to their
webs to start a new day ...
          Emily (10)

Bear fishing

Fish swim peacefully in
   the water,
meandering in a line.
I dream of the silvery
   scales slithering down
      my throat.
  I taste the fresh fish
    cold on my tongue.
       My soft paws awaken the
       stillness of the water
     as I stare into the fish's skin.
  I feel a sharp pain
  as the freezing water
breaks up the warmth
  in me.
I can remember the first
  time I had fish.
It was brought back in my
  mother's tender mouth.
  I bit into it
  and I felt like I was
    born again.
          Catherine (10)

This is work by children who are used to the arts. They have worked, since they were small, in one of two classrooms separated by a wall which contains a stained glass window representing wildlife on the reservoir near the school. The present headteacher commissioned and bought this window when other schools were spending money on the filing cabinets deemed necessary to contain the paraphernalia of the National Curriculum. The children regularly visit the Sainsbury Arts Centre at the University of East Anglia in Norwich, and have close contact with the artist Dale Devereux Barker, and the dancer Michael Platt.

They are also used to my work with them. I have visited this school for three to six mornings every year for the last nine years, and each time I come back the children seem to need less priming, less preparatory work: they are ready to go, to write with an unusual vigour about whatever I set before them. I might as well add that, although they live within six miles of the centre of Ipswich in Suffolk, they are rural children. These poems are, unusually for this book, second drafts, because the headteacher Duncan Allan has worked with the children on their work after my visit.

There is, of course, melodrama in Sally's poem. This is excusable in a young writer, as I have written before; to go over the top is necessary in order to learn restraint. More importantly, the children are learning about themselves, exploring in the animals their own experiences. Children use the distance that writing about animals gives them to write about just-glimpsed aspects of themselves. This is especially true at the end of Catherine's poem: 'I can remember the first / time I had fish. / It was brought back in my / mother's tender mouth. / I bit into it / and I felt like I was / born again'. Hughes may well be writing about part of himself in his poem. He may be a hawk. Catherine may well still be a baby bear.

Sophie Chipperfield, who teaches poetry (amongst, of course, everything else) with a remarkable passion, sent me some poems that had been written under the influence of something written by my son. His poem had been published in a collection of award-winning entries from the 1993 W H Smith Young Writers' Competition. He had written of a cat: 'I am the lolling, curled up in the chair / in the airing cupboard … / I am the dragging of dead thrushes / across the garden … '

This is a useful structure, apparently:

Black widow

I am the waiting, as the wind blows,
I am the venom, injecting my catch,
I am the treachery, eating my kind,
I am the darkening, the black of day.

I am the legs, two times four,
flash,
the run, the catch,
the rush of adrenaline.

I am the widow that eats her husband,
the creeping the queen of hiding.
The making of thread so fine.
I am the silence, stiffness, stillness.

I am the death,
the bite, the black,
the feasting of flies,
the horror, the pain, the triumphant.

Adam H (11)

I am the prints in the sandy dust
in the grass
in the path
on the path
behind closed doors.

I am the ball in the corner
in the warm
in the cold
I am the squeaking that pierces the night.

I am the neglected thing in the corner.
People flash by but never stop
time to time.

Jenny (10)

Footnote: Some haiku and some riddles

I asked these children to write loose haiku (according to the *Longmans Concise English Dictionary*, that is the plural as well as the singular) about the planets. We decided not to keep to the strict syllabic count, but to try to write tiny poems capturing some aspect of each planet:

Venus

Spectacular, sparkling Venus
spinning like a miraculous
misty moon.

Alice (10)

Earth

Earth is a huge sphere
with one moon like a mirror.
We roam its surface.

Greville (10)

Jupiter

Biggest planet
famous for its big red spot.
Why doesn't it put some cream on it?
It's getting kind of public.

Jennifer (9)

Saturn

A big ball playing
hula hoop with its rainbow
rings, beyond Jupiter.

Laura (10)

Uranus

Unique Uranus
striped with shadows of wondrous blue
frozen with its beauty.

Alice (10)

Pluto

Cold snowball in space
god of the dead, cold, icy.
One breath and lights out.

There is more about haiku and other poems using syllabic counts in Chapter 10.

The Anglo-Saxon riddles preserved in the *Exeter Book* (Crossley-Holland 1979) represent, probably, the strongest part of an English poetic tradition. Crossley-Holland has written about this form of poem that these 'misleading descriptions and mind-bending word-play' are 'powerful' because they contain 'secrets'. And 'if you can answer a riddle its power is your power because you have become the guardian of the secret'. The riddle is powerful in teaching for another reason. As Crossley-Holland tells us, the word comes from the Anglo-Saxon 'raedan' which means to teach or instruct, and by means of jokes, puns and catch questions, a riddle teaches us about the subject of the riddle and the language in which the riddle is framed. It teaches us to look: we end as we began with the principle of **observation**.

We have playfulness and versatility in riddles too. Some examples:

Riddle

I have twenty-eight faces,
    fifty-six ears.
Some parts of me are happy
    and some are close to tears.

Parts of me are topped with gold,
    parts with brown.
I'm a strange, many-headed creature
    in a strange town.

Alternative first stanza, less unhappy:

I have twenty-eight faces,
    fifty-six eyes.
Some parts of me are happy
    and some are full of sighs.

Fred Sedgwick

(*Answer: a class of children*)

We are five little airy creatures,
All of different voice and features,
One of us in glass is set;
One of us you'll find in jet;
T'other you may see in tin;
And the fourth a box within;
If the fifth you should pursue,
It can never fly from you.

Jonathan Swift

(*Answer: the vowels*)

There are some excellent collections of riddles as well as the *Exeter Book* to which I
have already referred; probably the best is *The New Exeter Book of Riddles* edited by
Kevin Crossley-Holland and Lawrence Sail.

Children's riddles

I go round and round
up and down
left and right
backwards and forwards.

(*electricity*)

Kevin (10)

I am a peach
that you can't touch.
I burn your eyes
if you look at me.

(*sun*)

Kimberley (9)

I'm round,
one screw
in the ear
like Frankenstein

(*clock*)

Holly (10)

'Frankenstein' should, of course, be 'Frankenstein's Monster'.

A young writer whom I had met on a course sent me the following riddles. She told me later that her class had had to write music about the elements. Her group had been allocated fire, and she wrote that riddle first. ('I read a fiction book about fire … '):

I am an artist,
A cook and a magician;
A burning god or
A captured slave;
I am the craftsman,
The watchman,
The raging warrior
And the quiet decoration.
I am the caring father
And the indifferent youth;
   I am fire,
     Ignis.

I am a historian,
A gardener and a farmer,
A throaty orator or
A jangling gypsy;
I am the caterer,
The mother,
The towering immortal
And the humble labourer.
I am the gentle saint
And the merciless enemy.
   I am Earth,
     Terra.

I am a dancer,
A mystic and idealist,
A luring siren or
An innocent Amazon;
I am the dreamer,
The wanderer,

The mourning widow
And the sallying lover;
I am the ruthless beast
And the silent conjurer,
    I am air,
        Aer.

I am a diviner,
A nurse and a provider,
A hearty sailor or
A gushing maiden;
I am the musician,
The singer,
The bantering child
And the furious foe;
I am the steely destroyer
And the crouching beggar;
    I am water,
        Aqua.

                        Eloise (11)

Conclusion

Obviously, I do not suggest that we can teach all science – all its content, all its method – through poetry. I do believe though, and hope that I have demonstrated, that we can begin with poetry in teaching the critical principle for both disciplines of observation, and thereby help children to look both more creatively and more respectfully at the world in which they live.

Prose interlude
Children and their names

I have written before (Sedgwick 1994c) that

> a central thread in PSME is how we can teach each other to face realities, and how we accept that facing up to anything is never easy ...

PSME (Personal, Social and Moral Education) is learning and teaching each other about the moral centres of our existence, both in private terms and in public ones and, even more importantly, in the place where private and public run up against each other. It is problematic as a subject, and therefore frequently over-simplified into audits of travel skills, health skills, drug problems and the like. What follows here are strategies based on writing designed to enhance our teaching and learning in this area.

'A gem I am going to keep forever'

Children and names

> '... and whatsoever Adam called every living creature, that was the name thereof ...'
>
> Genesis 2:19 (Authorized Version)

I am going to introduce a subject – names – that children write well about in prose rather than poetry. This is not being perverse. Two values of good prose – clarity and rhythm – are values of poetry as well. Fine poets who cannot write lucid prose are few in number. Indeed, what commonly distinguish inadequate prose in newspapers – pretentiousness, obscurity, cliché, verbosity, a slipshod attitude to style (all of which, among other things, are part of an evident refusal to re-read and revise before submitting work to an editor) also distinguish inadequate poetry. So prose writing is a useful skill for young poets to practise. It is one skill with which writers can show their respect for the rest of the human race, because no well-disposed person will bore or irritate his or her readers.

I will go further. It is useful to practise prose outside the usual story genre. For some reason, ever since I can remember, 'write a story about it' has been a ubiquitous and insistent demand in primary schools. This demand has been made often when narrative is not required, but reportage, or merely revision, or even repetition of historical or scientific facts. 'Story' is frequently an inappropriate word. Even when genuine narratives are required, with plot, characterization, craftiness and an awareness of what can be done with time in a story, little effort is put into teaching the basics of narrative writing.

This chapter grew slowly and insistently from a remark by an eleven-year-old student, Hannah, who was on a course I was teaching. I will print her writing later. 'I've come here' she said (in answer to my question) 'so I can write better essays'. I was taken aback. What an old-fashioned word 'essay' is, I remember thinking, both in the context of education (who writes essays these days?), and in the context of literature (I thought of the odd term 'belles-lettrism'). But it struck me that 'essay' might be a useful word. It means 'to try, to put to the proof ... to test the nature ... to attempt' (*Shorter Oxford English Dictionary*). 'Try', 'proof', 'test', 'attempt' ... these are good educational words. All poetry writing is 'an experiment with a yes and a no answer' as Miroslav Holub said in a interview. These essays can be seen as experiments with prose aimed at understanding our names and our relationship to them, and the other relationships moving constantly around us that they imply: those with our parents and grandparents, and other people after whom we have been named.

Adults and children have understood for thousands of years the importance of names. A Cherokee chant, quoted in *The Puffin Book of Magic Verse* (chosen by Charles Causley, 1974), begins:

> Listen!
> I have come to step over your soul
> I know your clan
> I know your name ...

This rhyme implies that knowledge of a name brings power. Indeed, we know, or sense, that we own part of someone when we have discovered their 'handle'. This slang word suggests that we can manipulate fellow human beings when we can call them something. This is why introductions are so important at parties, and why we are embarrassed when we forget someone's name, or fed up when they forget ours. We know this is true in a less cheerful part of everyday life. Watch a policeman taking down a motorist's details, or listen to a teacher correcting some child's mis-behaviour, using, like Tom Sawyer's loving but fierce Aunt Polly, the child's full name. A teacher, Liz, told me on a course that she always associated 'Elizabeth' with a reprimand.

This importance should not surprise us. Adam named the animals to make them his. 'Whatsoever Adam called every living creature, that was the name thereof' (Genesis 2:19). We take great care over the naming of our children, and even our pets. Look for a moment at how Dickens named his characters. In one novel, *David Copperfield*, he invented and named Steerforth, with its strength in 'forth' and its hint of manipulativeness in 'steer'; Murdstone with its double helping of deathly coldness and cruelty; and Peggotty, as redolent as any name could be of pure good nature.

Very young children glimpse something of the importance of names when they decide what their soft toys are to be called. I remember a cuddly dog that I won for my toddler son in a competition at a school fair. Instantly he called it 'Ernest Brown Ernest Bagwoof' and it has kept that name for sixteen years. Even now that he is eighteen, and between school and the worlds of work and college, even though he goes to rock concerts with his mates in big parks, even though he drinks beer in pubs, and works in hotels abroad without his parents, EBEB is still on his bed, ignored, certainly, but with an important and named presence. It is not time yet to throw him out. And there never will be such a time, because EBEB will probably be handed on to my son's children. His name still has a profound significance – for him and for his parents, and for his memories of his childhood; for his stories about himself, and his stories about him. And it will probably be significant for a future generation.

Names matter because they say so much about our parents and their times, and what they hoped for on our behalf. My own given name speaks about an Edwardian past. In some parts of the world, names are even more significant: they give away allegiances. To restrict my examples to the British Isles (a significant and politically charged name itself) Patricks and Siobhans in Belfast or Derry are likely to be on a different side of a tragic old fence from Williams and Elizabeths. Indeed, Ulster people tell us what side they are on simply by naming the city. Is it Derry or Londonderry?

All over these islands, Victorias, Virginias, Graces and Fredericks ('peaceful ruler') carry moral burdens from their naming. Other names speak about newness, about being up to date. Hence those names that come from soap operas and professional footballers. The power of names is demonstrated yet again when we meet (as I did recently) a ten-year-old Arnold, to be told that the boy had been named after Arnold Schwarzenegger. The teacher who told me this had a look of barely suppressed moral superiority on her face, and I reckon my face mirrored it. Only a name could generate such smugness. Names are important, too, because to name someone, as all of us who are parents know, is a creative act. At a lower level, Auden put it like this: 'Imagination is the ability to name cats'.

I have been talking with children about their names, and have discovered that, given the opportunity, they reflect creatively on them. A six-year-old, for example, once asked 'Why did God call me Joanna?' (see my 1999 book *Thinking About Literacy*, Routledge) and a colleague told me that she remembered skipping in her front garden as a child saying 'I am Jenny Taylor and I am five and I am here'. Both these children were reflecting in unmeasurable ways, not only on their names, but on their respective places in the world and, in the first case, on a relationship with God.

In the related beliefs that, first, poetry begins with words, not ideas or thoughts, and, second, that at some stage everyone's most significant word is their given name, I have, over the past few months, been asking children questions about their names, and showing them games they can play with those names:

- Do you like your name?
- Are you named after anyone?
- Or do you know any other reason why you have your name?
- Who gave you your name?
- Do you know what your name means?
- Does anything annoy you about your name?

One unsurprising but important fact emerges clearly. Children hate having fun made of their names. 'Patience is a virtue, / Virtue is a grace; / And Grace is a little girl / Who doesn't wash her face' (Opie, Opie and Sendak 1992). This rhyme goes down badly with Graces, I know, and Patiences, I suspect. Holly, who was born four days before Christmas, and given, therefore, a seasonal name, 'hates it when my Mum says "I will hang you on the wall"'. Hannah doesn't like being called Spanner, though Anna, who 'hates' her name (this isn't an easy area) *prefers* Spanner. Tom is fed up with being called 'The Tank Engine'. In another generation, he would probably have been called 'The Piper's Son'. Danielle, who likes her name, is called Dazzy by her friends, which is fine by her, but she hates it 'when my Dad keeps saying it in a droning-on girl's voice'.

I labour this point, because for years teachers have made classroom jokes about, or of, children's names, probably causing more discomfort than they knew. Like the Holly example above, it seems innocent. To the child it often isn't. As an adult, I dislike it when children call me (and they often do) Fred Flintstone, or tell me their hamster is called Fred.

Children also hate people writing or saying their names inaccurately. Aaron and Rachael were two examples of children who don't like their names because 'people get them wrong'. As someone who has had to spell his surname tens of thousands of times in shops and over the phone to try to stop people giving me an irritating redundant 'e' in the middle, I know how they feel. Visiting the infant school where I was enrolled as a five-year-old, I found that the secretary or headteacher had spelt my name incorrectly in the admissions register all those years ago. Children understand intuitively that it is a basic mark of respect to get a name right. To know someone's name, but to know it wrong, is to care, but not enough. It is to possess some part of someone incomplete, or damaged in a small but significant way. Say what you like about me, Reader, but spell my name right.

Girls often don't like what they see as traditional 'feminine' names: Rebecca (10) said 'I don't like my name because it is too girlish'. Some names take on new meanings that hurt children. One Camilla slightly (but understandably) confused, said 'I am not named after that princess'. Anna (9) says 'I don't like my name, it is babyish'. Some children carry with them jokes about their names.

Children who have been named after a person, and who have been told the story, are usually proud. Luke was named after the Gospel-writer, and likes that, adding 'I am also named after Luke Skywalker'. Christopher was named after Christopher Lee the actor, and enjoyed being told the legend of Offero, his original namesake, who carried Christ across a river one stormy night, and gained a rich addition to his name as a result ('Christoffero'). Alexandra was named after the hospital she was born in. Unusually, she knew what her name meant: it is 'helpful' in Greek. Rose (6) likes her name and writes 'I'm named after a flower'. Mary Jane liked her name, and tells me that she is named 'after Spiderman's girlfriend'. Arnie (7) liked his name. He was called, like someone who appeared earlier, after Arnold Schwartzenegger, and thinks, reasonably enough, that it is a 'tough and strong' name.

How open the very fact of talking about names makes these children! They say things about love and hate, about parents and other ancestors, about heroes their parents might have had before they were born, that they would never say unless they had been asked to talk about their names.

I carry with me, on my visits to schools, the *Wordsworth Dictionary of First Names* edited by Isaebail Macleod and Terry Freedman (Wordsworth 1995) so that I can tell children what their names mean. I learn from it that Paul comes from the Latin word for 'small', that Pamela means 'honeyed sweetness' ('though two ex-husbands wouldn't agree' said Pamela the literacy adviser in one authority, intriguingly); that, in Greek Zoe is 'life' and Sophie 'wisdom'; that in Hebrew Rebecca is, oddly 'clip' or 'thing that binds' and Rachel 'ewe'. There is an even better dictionary, Eric Partridge's *Traditional First Names*, also published by Wordsworth, too bulky for my travelling jobbing poet kit.

Unfortunately, these books don't deal with that relatively recent phenomenon in our society, the prominence of Asian names. We need a more inclusive dictionary that welcomes all Mohammeds and Fatimas, all Pritams and Kim Pans. Because names are huge clues to our racial, cultural and religious identification, when we read to children poems that use only western Judaeo-Christian names, this effectively excludes children from marginalized cultural backgrounds. Such children are so used to this, they barely notice the fact. I use two poems to try to bring excluded children into the name discussion. The first is by Judith Nicholls, and is called 'Name this child':

> Joginder, Gurbachan or Amrit,
> Ravinder, Rajinder, Swaran,
> Satpal, Surinder or Manjit,
> Paramjit, Kirpal or Pritam?
>
> Leela, Vaneela or Tara,
> Ravi, Rajeesh or Rajan,
> Sandeep, Gopal or Tushar,
> Sushila, Manjula, Poonam?
>
> Gulab, Hussain, Zubaida,
> Parveen, Shamin or Hassan,
> Jamila, Sharif or Farida,
> Nasima, Nasrat, Shazadan?

Van Choc or Van Thai or Thi Kim,
Ken Tsong or Ka Win or Yuk Fan,
Thi My or Van Khai or Thi Thien,
Lai Ling or Lai Ching or Kim Pan?

Jessica, Jocelyn, Lavinia,
Mildred, Matilda or Anne,
Herbert or Humphrey or Hubert,
Letitia, Patricia, Diane?

Judith Nicholls, reproduced by permission of the author.
Published in *Collins Primary Poetry no. 3* 'You're Late' edited by Fred Sedgwick

Here is a suggestion for teachers and children: make up a poem like this one, in four or five stanzas. Each stanza must be composed of names; the first, names from a certain category of your life, the second from a different one, and so on. Read it to a friend, and see how resonant it is – first to you, and then after conversation to your friend.

The other poem that is inclusive rather than exclusive is my own piece in honour of Asian food. It is a delight to watch the faces of children from Asian and near Eastern cultures light up as they hear the words in this poem, and to watch the expressions of white children change as they see words that originate from a different culture from their own becoming – for once – the centre of attention. Admittedly, these names aren't children's names, but they are arguably the next best thing: names of food.

Mr Khan's Shop
is dark and beautiful.
There are parathas,

garam masala,
naan breads full of fruit.

There are bhajees, samosas, dhal,
garlic, ground cumin seeds.

Shiny emerald chillies
lie like incendiary bombs.

There are bhindi in sacks,
aloo to eat with hot puris

and mango pickle. There's
rice, yoghurt,

cucumber and mint –
raitha to cool the tongue.

Sometimes you see
where the shop darkens

Mr Khan, his wife
and their children

round the table.
The smells have come alive.

He serves me
pappadums, smiles,

re-enters the dark.
Perhaps one day

he'll ask me to dine with them:
bhajees, samosas, pakoras,

coriander, dhal.
I'll give him this poem: *Sit down*

young man, he'll say
and eat your words.

from my collection *Blind Date*, 1999a

By including this poem in my book, I am trying to make the point that names are powerful, and names of foods especially so. They are basic names, resonant of the essentials of a people. They are like the names of bread or, more importantly, beer (bière, Bier, birra, cerveza, ol, bir – since you ask, in French, German, Italian, Spanish, Swedish and Yiddish, respectively) or the names of rivers. Say Ouse, Nile, Mississippi, Avon, Ganges, Dordogne, Po, Thames – and then say them again, but this time out loud. Both river names and food names speak about what we are and what we need, of what we could not do without, of what sustains us. To talk about these names in a classroom is to talk about our individual and racial identities, and it is also to honour those identities.

I have found, in INSET (In-Service Education for Teachers) sessions for educators – teachers, classroom assistants, nursery nurses, learning support workers – that one way of breaking the ice is to present everyone with large pieces of sugar paper (one between each group of four or five), and to ask people to choose a colour of felt-tip pen, and to write their first name the way they sign it, and tell stories to the other members of a five- or six-strong group. The colour of the pen is important, because it might give something away about politics or background. I start, to show that I don't mind being open about this. I always choose green or red.

I talk about how I've disliked my name – whether Frederick, Fred or Freddie – since I was small. I talk about how I still find it embarrassing when being introduced to strangers, as if I was Cyril or Cecil or Norbert. It was my father's name. He was still away in Asia during the war. I was born in 1945, and my name was given to me without much thought by my mother while she was recovering from my birth. Surrounded by Catholic nuns who had told her (she assured me later) that I would go to limbo (a notion totally foreign to her then, as it is to me now) if I died unnamed, she could only think of her distant husband's Christian names and her own maiden name. What a moment that must have been to her. She must have thought for some time and with some intensity of this new life in her arms, and that other life at risk on the other side of the world. Frederick Reginald Byers Sedgwick ... This is the first time I have owned up to this baggage, and to the fact that my mother's panicking unpreparedness became increasingly typical of her to me as I grew up.

So I disliked my name. 'Fred' was out of date when I was a child in the 1950s. The other boys were called Graham, Peter, Michael and John, and I envied them. My younger brother had acquired the more 'normal' Colin. Then one day, a few years ago, playing with the list at the end of Webster's *Third New International Dictionary* that gives translations in six languages of English words, I discovered that Fred is the Swedish word for 'peace'. My name was redeemed! It had emerged as the operative word in phrases like 'peace and quiet' and 'the peace that passeth all understanding': desirable, beautiful and profound.

I tell this story, and then ask teachers to tell theirs. I have heard illuminating tales doing this: of a nun, for example, who was called Sister Scholastica because her name was picked with a pin from a book of saints; of a woman who changed her name from Dorothy to Kate as a student, and, miraculously, made the change stick (I tried to be Michael for few weeks once in the late 1960s); of a Jo who longed to be Joanna because it sounded 'posher'; of a Len who wouldn't tell us his first name – Len was his second, and the only one he'd own up to; of a Theresa who is called Tess only by her husband, and then only to 'wind me up'; of a Mia, whose father wanted to call her Maria after a previous girlfriend, and whose mother agreed, amazingly, to a truncated version of her predecessor's name; of a Shansa, who was named after the Hindi word for lightning. As I listened to teachers talking about their names during this exercise, I could see friendships begin and grow as the process of the early understanding of each other is beguilingly accelerated, and as the importance of naming is underlined.

Here are some children writing about their names; first, some infants. These pieces can hardly be called essays, of course, but building blocks for essays that might or might not be written another time. They might be more usefully considered as little objects made by the writers to help them reflect on themselves, their names, and the people who gave them those names:

> I like my name because my mum likes it and my dad named me after Luke Skywalker and I like my name and I was named after Saint Luke who wrote the gospel.
>
> Luke (6)

> I do not like my name Christopher because it is too long. My name is a bit famous because a giant helped a child across a deep river. My nickname is Christi More. My middle name is Gary. I was named after my Dad. I would like to be named Gary because it is short.
>
> Christopher (6)

I was called Mahmiri because I was named after my Grandma. My cousin calls me Mickey Too and I don't like it. It always annoys me so I ignore them. All my cousins call me Joanne.

Mahmiri (6)

I like my name because it means Christ. I was called Christy because it's near crystal, bright shining and pretty. My nickname is sometimes Chrissy. When people take the Mickey out of me they call me Fiddler. I like my middle name Lauren because it reminds me of lollipops.

Christy (6)

I like my name because I am named after my Grandad and some people call me Saunders and some people call me Thomas George and I also like that they call me that.

Thomas (6)

Looking closely at these notes, several things emerge. One is the contentment that shines from some of them. If his writing about his names is anything to go by (and it must be at least partly significant) Thomas seems to have a life neatly (so far) arranged. He is happy with whatever he is called. Second, there are strange reasons for not liking names: 'because it is too long', for example. Frequently, other children didn't like their names 'because they were common' (meaning, I think 'frequent' rather than 'vulgar') or 'because no one else is called it'. Third, children are often acutely aware of the name's significance: 'it means Christ. I was called Christy because it's near crystal, bright shining and pretty ... ' A six-year-old called Paige seemed ready to defend her name straightaway: 'I was called Paige because both my Mum and Dad like it'. I felt she had been gently challenged about her name already. Fathers' jokes and obsessions have much to answer for. Chelsea tells me that she was named 'after my Dad's football team' and Amber has been handed down an old family joke. She was named 'after a traffic light'.

The next writer was ten years old:

My name

My name is Shixin [pronounced, roughly – sorry, Shixin – Shiz-*in*]. It comes from Singapore, because that is where my Mum used to live. I have forgotten what it means, but I do know that when it is written in Chinese you can change it so that it sounds the same, but means 'Die, heart'.

My Mum was going to call me Shewonsing but when someone tried to pronounce it, it sounded like 'She won't sing' so my Mum decided to change it.

I used to dislike my name but when I found out what it could be changed to, I decided it wasn't so bad.

As far as I know, there is only one other person called Shixin, and she owns a restaurant called Shixin. Some people tried to give me a nickname, but it was hard, because not a lot of things rhyme with Shixin.

My Dad wanted to call me Bonnie after *Bonnie and Clyde* (a film) but my Mum would have none of it, so that is how I got my middle name, Bonnie. I'm not sure if this is true, because my brother told me, and sometimes he tells lies. His name is Shi-Hacon. Shi is my Mum's surname, so she put it at the front of our names. In a way, I have two surnames! I also have two middle names.

My second middle name is Grace, which means 'love of God'.

My full name is: Shixin Bonnie Grace Bickerton.

Finally, Hannah, who is eleven, wrote an essay about her name, summing up much of our positive feelings:

My name

Some people dislike their names, but I don't. I think it is unusual and interesting. I think you should treasure your name. It shows who you are.

I am not named after anyone but I don't mind. It's fine to have a name to myself, if you know what I mean. My name means 'God has favoured' and I think that is a beautiful meaning.

My mother chose my name. I don't know why. It was just one of those things.

My nickname is completely different. I get called Chicken. This is because when I was younger we went to a zoo and there were lots of animals running around and I got scared so ever since Dad has called me Chicken.

I am not going to change my name. Your name is precious like a gem and I am going to keep it forever.

Since the beginning of this chapter, I have been travelling along prose paths rather than poetic ones. But the signposts in the country have all been pointing to aspects of poetry: clarity, rhythm, avoidance of cliché, and, above all, an experimental interest in what we are as human beings, down to the names that are part of our roots. Much as someone who doesn't care what he or she eats doesn't care about anything, no one who lacks an interest in his or her name will write poetry.

At a lower level, the practice of writing clear prose is good practice for writing poems. There is a sub-romantic idea that poetry doesn't need the basic rules of grammar, manners and sense, but only the truly great can afford to break those rules with any regularity. Most poetry requires correct, even conventional grammar, and e.e. cummings' agenda (he despised capital letters so much that he didn't use them, even for his own name) is never ours unless we want to ape him. And we don't want to ape any writer.

The idea that grammar and conventional spelling are there to be flouted because one is an artist is related to the equally dopy notion that poetry can use defunct words like 'sojourned' for 'lived', as in 'I sojourned in that fair academic town [Cambridge – this is a real example from an adult poem] for years'. Such a sentence would be absurd in prose, where a ground rule is to use the language you would speak to respected human beings in. It would be laughable in conversation. It is

Lottie Coleman   St. Nicholas House
My Name

My name is Charlotte and it is shortened to Lottie. This is because my mum only called me Charlotte because she could call me Lottie.

I dislike my name but don't hate it. It's not what I would have chosen.

My name is the female version of Charels. It means woman.

My second name is my aunts second name. My first name, though, wasn't named after anyone.

I had a weird way about choosing my name because my mum stuck names on the fridge and saw which one suited me. There was Harriet, Belinda and Charlotte so I think I ended up with the nicest name out of the three!

13 My name – child's writing

almost certainly absurd in verse, unless used with a tuned sense of mockery, and enormous, justified confidence.

Later, I introduced Hannah and her friends to an old game that I first heard in a playground in Slough ten years ago. Since then, I have found that all children like playing it with their names. W H Auden once said that anyone who would be a writer has first of all to have a need to play with language. What better words to play with than our own given names!

> Hannah bom bannah
> stick a lannah fi fannah
> fi fannah stick a lannah
> that's how you spell Hannah.

It works with even the most difficult names:

> Arabella bom barabella
> sticka larabella fi farabella
> fi farabella sticka larabella
> That's how you spell Arabella.

as well as easy ones:

> Paul bom baul
> sticka laul fi faul
> fi faul sticka laul
> That's how you spell Paul.

Look at the power of names in this writing. I have left it unedited as the author's racy style reflects what she is saying.

> I come from a very strange family, if you ask me! My Sicilian Nana and Grandad had 7 kids, my Dad (Joe) my Auntie Anna, my uncle Luca, my uncle Tony, my uncle Ben, my uncle Carmelo and my uncle Gasparo. Now my Auntie Anna has married to my uncle Peter and they had four kids, Rosa, Pasquale, Franca and Enza. Rosa got married in July to Tony Belivia and now she's expecting a baby in July. Pasquale has married … They split up but now theyre back together again. Franca is still single but the best of the lot, Enza, is married to a bloke called James. My uncle Luca had two kids. I think, I don't know, but I think theyre both married. My dad has got four kids. My brother Enzo, my brother Tony and me. And my half-brother Luca. My Uncle Ben married my Auntie Margaret and they had a kid Franscesca. They had a premature child, Anna, and it died. My uncle Tony married my auntie Josepina they had one child called Vincenzo and shes expecting a child. My uncle Carmelo married my auntie Carol they have got two children Vincenzo 13 and Mario 8 months, my uncle Garspare married my auntie Luca and they had a child called Vinezo, 23, and Franca 21 and they had a boy but he died then they had another girl called Uta-Maria.
> My nanna and grandad are now in there 70s but are still a laugh but my grandad looks like Hitlar when he was older so whenever we see him when we

are talking we say "Hitlar" and we run as fast as we can. I think we are a very big family.

Everyone's name is interesting. The names in that piece of prose might suggest that only the exotic arrests us. But **poetry, like names, is a democratic subject.**

Eloise, who is the eleven-year-old writer of the element riddles on p.57–8, and a self-generating writer, sent the following, the only example in this book, I think, of what is called light verse:

> I wish I had a normal name
> Like Alison or Jane.
> I'd have any sort of name
> If only it were plain.
> I wish I had a normal name
> Like Sarah or Tess.
> The only thing I want in life
> Is a normal name (more or less).
> I have a sister called Alice
> And a brother named Paul
> But when you are called Justine-Therese
> I'd rather not have a name at all.
> I wish I had a normal name
> Like Carla or Kate.
> When I'm older I will change my name.
> Till then I'll have to wait.
>
> Eloise (11)

Part II

Poetry and Personal, Social and Moral Education

5 Me and the rest of the world

'My box is made of people. It is a human box'

Perry (10)

What is PSME? In its broadest sense it is everything we can possibly conceive of, whether in our learning or in our teaching. At its best, it is a curriculum that accepts that 'the closer you get into your own nerves, the closer you get to what's universal' (Chambers 1986); and that the closer you get to the universal, the closer you get to your own nerves. It is a curriculum that accepts that the internal and the external are yoked together, and that our understanding of one goes in pace with our understanding of the other. (I would insist that we can't learn without teaching, but suspect that is a story for another time and another place.) Admittedly, some subjects seem to fit best in the 'personal' part – creative writing, painting, to take two examples – while others fit best into the social part – geography, say, and history. But in fact, all subjects fall into both parts. How can you consider a tribe living in Australasia, or in Ancient Greece, without considering yourself and your place in the world? How can you write or paint without thinking about everything that is around you?

Some formulations of the idea prefer to put in 'Health' where I have put 'Moral', but I prefer it my way because the subject, or, more accurately, the theme (PSME transcends, or underpins all mere subjects) is, at its deepest place, concerned with justice and fairness. What (PSME asks) is the good life? The good life, that is, in the way we pray and meditate and think on our own, and the way in which our prayers, our thoughts, our meditations affect our friends and enemies, and, of course, vice versa. I recognize that 'the nature of morality is deeply problematical' (White 1990) and that, therefore, to teach it we have to help children formulate their notions of the good life rather than impose ours on them. The 'Health' formulation all too readily reduces PSME to audits of things children have to 'cover' in their schooling – smoking, alcohol, travel competence, drugs education – rather than widening the issues to what we are and ought to be.

A simple way to begin to teach basic Personal, Social and Moral Education to five-year-olds is to ask them for a list of good things that their friend does for them.

It is important here to recognize that **there is more than one way to compose than writing things down**. These infants are making poems as their teachers act as secretaries:

My friend
helps me to get food for the cat.

My friend
tidies my room with me.
My friend
plays action man cars with me.

Me and my friend
talk about how we grow.

My friend
plays football with me.
My friend
sleeps with me.
My friend
helps to pick me up.
Me and my friend
talk about how we grow.
My friend
plays on my climbing frame.
My friend
sits next to me.
My friend
likes me.
Me and my friend
talk about how we grow.

My friend
visits me at my house.
My friend
loves me.
My friend
helps me to skip.
Me and my friend
talk about how we grow.

My friend
gives me sweets.
My friend
goes with me to the forest.
I go round my friend's.

Me and my friend
talk about how we grow.

My friend
cuddles me.
My friend
helps me to feed my fish.
My friend
helps me to feed my rabbit.
Me and my friend
talk about how we grow.

My friend
runs round the shops with me and back.
Me and my friend
talk about how we grow.

Infants do what they have always done: follow each other's ideas. Someone says, for example, 'My friend plays football with me' and someone else inevitably follows up with, 'My friend plays action man cars with me'. Teachers often roll their eyes upwards when this happens. In the classroom, it gets me down, too. How can one get across that children, however young, when faced with the problems of writing, have to be original? But plagiarism is always a problem with the inexperienced poet, and if children of five or six years old are not inexperienced poets, who is? And indeed, T S Eliot recommended plagiarism when he said somewhere that the great poet actually steals ideas.

But it is also clear here that infants say surprising things. Look at that wonderful line: 'Me and my friend talk about how we grow'. Of course, once we think of it, we understand that all children reflect on growth: babyhood, infancy, childhood, adolescence, adulthood, middle age, old age and death. But here someone has made it pleasingly explicit for us and has made us think: perhaps we ought to make the idea of growth central to our thinking. I chose this line as a line worthy of being repeated at the end of each stanza, each group of lines. Normally, I would work to the end that the children should chose the repeating line themselves, but on this occasion there was no time to do that.

I printed several copies of these words on the computer, and handed some round to the children, put one on the wall, and sent one to the headteacher with the optimistic request that it be shown to the governors. Thus the children's poem about their friends had been published. The PSME element here is two-fold: first the children were writing about (and therefore learning about) their friends, and their relationships with their friends, and the great thing they shared, growth; and second, their work was honoured by being published. This lesson was aimed at helping the children, collectively, to write a poem; but a critical by-product was improving their self-esteem, both as individuals, and as a class.

In another school, seven- and eight-year-olds did the same exercise

concentrating on their families. This time, the children wrote their own words
down, though some used secretaries as described above:

> My Mum does the housework
> My Grandad lets me have sweets
> My Nana asks how I did with my spellings
> My Mum lets me play out the front
> When my sister falls over I ask her if she is OK
> My Nanny lets me ride on her horses
> My friend says you're my bestest friend.
> My Dad says you're my best girl at Mathematics
> My friend says you draw good
>
> > Salina

> I laugh when my Dad tickles me on the tummy
> On holiday it was Halloween and my brother dressed up as a dead rat.
>
> > Yasmin

Writing about anger

> I was angry with my friend
>
> > Blake

Poetry has more to contribute to PSME than any other subject. I have suggested in
my book (1994c) that PSME is critical in helping children with vital issues, the
great guns in the armoury of art: birth and death; love, sex and relationships; good
and evil, peace and war and violence; hatred of people different from, and the same
as, ourselves. In my formulation, PSME is about respect for everyone and everything else. Poetry, as an engine in PSME, can help children to deal with their loves
and their passions. It can also help them to deal with negative feelings, such as
boredom, violence and depression. And their anger: this next writer has studied
Vasco Popa's 'Just come to my mind' (from 'Give me back my rags' in the *Collected
Poems*, 1978:54, and in *Junior Voices* (Summerfield 1970). Popa's poem mixes
things up in a very late twentieth-century way: thoughts scratch, eyes snarl, silence
punches and so on. These surreal images appeal to children because their language
has not yet been seduced by the dreaded common sense, by convention, by the
expected. Therefore they write well under Popa's influence:

> *Just come to my mind*
>
> Just come to my mind
> and my fingernails will shake the ground.
>
> Just come to my arm
> and the bones will break yours as if they were paper.

Just come to my hair
and it will punch you in the face.

Just come to my teeth
and they will electrocute you.
That's why I'm writing this.

                    Max (11)

Teachers have objected to this lesson. Some have said to me that it is 'unhealthy' that children should be encouraged to write about their most negative of feelings, their hate, because writing about hate might 'encourage' them to hate more. Others have been even less analytical, and said that they 'don't like that sort of work'. We are all capable of massive self-delusion, and I am reminded of a story that my friend Mary Jane Drummond told me: a girl on a playground says to the teacher on duty 'Maxie hit me, miss' and the teacher replies 'I'm sure she didn't'. Why do we pretend? Why are we sentimental about life as it is lived by both the children we teach and ourselves? All children are, sometimes, angry. Some children, for very good reasons – violence, abuse, unkindness, poverty – are angry most of the time. And are we not all capable of hate? We pretend, I suppose, because we are frightened of too much reality. 'The world is troubled / With a lack of looking' – I have already quoted George Tardios' words from Pirrie (1987) in my chapter on looking at objects. It is no less true when we are looking at our feelings and relationships, especially the darker, more disturbing ones that we would sooner pretend did not exist.

This poem was written after studying Popa's poem, too:

Hate Song

If you come into my sight
I'll tear your face to shreds
until you bleed to death.

If you come to have a fight with me
I'll pluck your hairs out
one by one.

If I have the slightest memory of you
I'll take your eyeballs out
and crumple them up
and then put them in.

Now you can see
how serious I am
about hating you!

                    Roseanne (10)

Popa's poem works well alongside these lines of William Blake's. Indeed, comparing Popa with Blake will lead to some interesting discussion about anger and the expression or suppression of it. Is it true that owning up to our anger with a friend ends it? That not owning up to anger with an enemy makes it worse? Is the expression of violent anger in a poem any different from its expression in speech, or a letter? Is it more justified?

> I was angry with my friend:
> I told my wrath, my wrath did end.
> I was angry with my foe:
> I told it not, my wrath did grow.
>
> And I water'd it in fears,
> Night & morning with my tears;
> And I sunned it with smiles,
> And with soft deceitful wiles.
>
> And it grew both day and night,
> Till it bore an apple bright;
> And my foe beheld it shine,
> And he knew that it was mine,
>
> And into my garden stole
> When the night had veil'd the pole:
> In the morning glad I see
> My foe outstretch'd beneath the tree.

I have forgotten how this next poem came to be written. But I remember the writer well. Its wild, surreal style was typical of her:

> As I slide off my sock
> and open every window in the house
> the puff goes miles.
>
> As I run fast
> my heart is beating
> like a copper penny.
>
> My eyes sting with anger –
> I'll get you for that!
>
> I'll take out my glass eye
> and throw it at you.
> Whizzz!
>
> Yes, and it will hit
> your big bum
>
> and it will be so red
> it will burn like a blazing fire.

You stick
I say in red anger.

All I get back,
not a stick,
but a great red tree trunk.

Stay away from him awhile.

I think my nose is so cold
it's going to drop off.
and all the snot in the world
I will throw at you.
I will give a big puff
and the world will stop turning.
Space will fall at my feet
and I will warm my snotty nose.

Danielle (10)

This is incoherent. But the medium is part of the message; anger is incoherent. And I agree with Barthes, when he writes that 'Incoherence seems to me preferable to a distorting order'. (1982)

Looking at this drawing, we can see how **the visual images that children make feed into their words, and vice versa.**

Young children write about anger, too:

> When I was angry my mummy wouldn't let me play on my Sega and I tried to get my own way. When it is bedtime I say Sorry Mummy and she says that's all right my sausage [the last phrase was originally written like this, identifiably Ipswich: 'tats arit my sasij'].

Writing about relatives

I have quoted from Christopher Smart's lines about his cat in Chapter 4. 'For I will consider' can be adapted for writing that helps children to celebrate their relationships with other people, as well as animals. I think it is worth re-reading Smart's lines at this point and the poems that children wrote (pp.39–41) so that we can begin to evaluate what Smart has done here in his presence in the classroom as a teacher: a teacher of language and a teacher of the emotions. The eccentric structures with which his free verse poem is built (heavily influenced, I think, by the rhythms of the Authorized Version of the Bible) have enabled the children (freed from the search for a structure themselves) to express emotions unsentimentally. This is even more true of the poems that follow:

> For I will consider my Mum
> with her long blonde wavy hair.

14 Child's angry face

For firstly she slouches down the farm house stairs.
For secondly she puts her lipstick on so carefully.
For thirdly she walks through the deep blue sea at four inches deep.
For fourthly she puts on her watch carefully so she won't scratch her tissued
    skin.

For fifthly she has to make her food with her pride and neatness
For sixthly she puts on her perfume with two or three sprays.
For seventhly she lies spreadly laid out while catching her brown tan from
    the hectic sun.
For eighthly she goes shopping and buys most of the best clothes ever.
For ninthly she puts on her hand lotion so daintily.
For tenthly she takes most pride in her appearance.
My Mum is very pretty in her ways and appearances.

Claire (9)

This writer uses words adroitly and freshly: 'hectic' in 'the hectic sun' is the best example. She has chosen 'spreadly', a coined adverb, and it should be left as it is. She expresses love with great tenderness and without sentimentality. 'Pride and neatness' captures more than I care to contemplate. After a few minutes' reflection, I realized she had achieved all this by two little twists of cleverness. First, she had not used the word 'love'. Brownjohn points out (1982) in *Does It Have To Rhyme?* that children write about colours more vividly when they have been told not to write the colours' names. It is a useful challenge to ask children to write about love without using the word. I must, sometime, ask children to write about death without using *that* word.

Second, this writer concentrates on objects that she associates with her mother, rather than her mother herself: lipstick, the sea, the watch that she puts on with such care because of her 'tissued skin', the hand lotion, 'the best clothes ever'. Thus, almost magically, these objects come to stand for the writer's mother and the relationship between them. This is a remarkable achievement. A clear picture of a woman emerges, of course; but more than that, we see an even clearer picture of a mother-daughter relationship.

I left the school feeling angry because the headteacher had told me that this girl had just failed the eleven-plus in her town, which retains selective schools. So she would be wearing, for the next few years, the black and white that identifies so-called failures there as sure as maroon and blue identifies so-called successes. We do not live in a society today that values emotional honesty, linguistic ability or poetry because, of course, they cannot be measured and examined.

Another girl wrote about 'her Uncle Graham'. This an eccentrically drawn portrait of an unemployed young man:

He wakes up with a long wide stretch.
He stamps downstairs.
He pours milk on his bread
and eats his milk and tries to drink his bread.
He turns the t.v. on, and sits down to see what's what.
He gets up with boredom and tramps back up the stairs.
He dresses and combs his bushy hair.
He pushes his bike out from the shed.
He rides away to Whitby near the sea ...

Another child wrote about her little sister:

> For firstly, she dresses, all in pink.
> For secondly, she eats her breakfast, as slow as a snail.
> …
> For thirdly she skips out the front door without doing her chores …
>
> Pamela (10)

Another way of writing about relatives is this: read them Angela Topping's poem 'My Best Friend' (in my anthology *Jenny Kissed Me*, Sedgwick 2000d). If you can't do this, know that the poem is simply a list of things that a loved grandfather does for a child, written with a sensitivity about line endings and stanzas and very subtle rhyme that children immediately appreciate. It is a spare poem that leaves the surprise of who the best friend is to the last line.

After reading this poem, Shane (the lines were arranged like this in his second draft) wrote:

> He stands with me in the
> dark while we watch bats
> fly about in the sky.
> We go on holiday.
> We visit crabs that
> crowd about like sea
> shells and sand.
> He says he loves me
> I love him he
> buys me toys
> like millennium bug
> he taught me
> the types of snakes
> like side winder
> and grass snake
> he stops me getting hurt
> I love my brother
>
> Shane (8)

Another writer in the same classroom wrote this poem:

> My best friend
> taught me
> how to say Dad and cow
> in African.
> We do things together
> like play board games
> such as Monopoly.

She buys me ear-rings
and when she went to Africa
she brought me back
a necklace made of wood and cow.
She taught me how
to flip a pancake
without
dropping it on
the floor.
I love my Aunty.

Sophie (9)

In another school, a child wrote this poem:

We sit together
as we stroke his cat.
We go for walks
near his house.

He is lonely
since his wife died
so we visit him often.
He comforts me
when I am upset.
He must know a lot
for he is interested in my work.
He is making a dinghy
for us to sail in.

He made me a wonderful stool
with a beaver on.
His house smells of coffee,
my grandpa.

Rebecca (8)

Extracts from other poems were:

We sit on the side of a pool / as she teaches me / names of flowers … She knows every animal by name / even snakes from Africa! … She taught me stories / of Jacob and his sons / She tells me who God is … He taught me how to enjoy life / To respect other people …

For another example of a poem written under the influence of Angela Topping's poem, see the end of this part of my book (p.108).

Gifts

There is a genre in English poetry (and, I should think, in other poetries) of the gift poem. This example is by Richard Corbet (1582–1635), and I found it in Gillian Avery's collection *The Everyman Anthology of Poetry for Children* (1994):

To his son, Vincent Corbet

What I shall leave thee, none can tell,
But all shall say I wish thee well:
I wish thee, Vin, before all wealth,
Both bodily and ghostly health;
Nor too much wealth, nor wit come to thee,
So much of either may undo thee.
I wish thee learning, not for show,
Enough for to instruct and know;
Not such as gentlemen require,
To prate at table or at fire ...
I wish thee peace in all thy ways,
Nor lazy nor contentious days;
And, when thy soul and body part,
As innocent as now thou art.

First, I just read the poem to the children, having practised it a few times. Then I asked them to tell me some of the things Corbet wants his son to have. Then I read this poem by Edward Thomas:

If ever I should by chance grow rich
I'll buy Codham, Cockridden and Childerditch,
Roses, Pyrgo, and Lapwater,
And let them all to my elder daughter.
The rent I shall ask of her will be only
Each year's first violets, white and lonely,
The first primroses and orchises –
She must find them before I do, that is.
But if she finds a blossom on furze
Without rent they shall for ever be hers,
Whenever I am sufficiently rich:
Codham, Cockridden and Childerditch,
Roses, Pyrgo, and Lapwater, –
I shall give them all to my elder daughter.

Notice that both these poems are composed simply of lists. The Edward Thomas is magical because of the use of place names, and the repetition of some of them at the end – 'Codham, Cockridden and Childerditch, Roses, Pyrgo, and Lapwater' –

makes for a satisfying rounded feeling to the poem. Why should not a list of places in our own lives have a similar resonance?

There are two lists in Thomas's poem: of places, and of the flowers that will be the rent he will ask of his daughter: 'violets, white and lonely, / The first primroses and orchises ... '

Then I suggested that the children close their eyes and think of someone they love: a baby brother or sister or cousin, or a child born down the road. What would you wish for that child?

To Helen

I will give you
the desert sand
as soft as a feather.

I will give you
the moonlight sky in India
and the silver stars.

I will give you
the mountains with the smooth rock.

I will give you
the sound of a humming bird
in a tropical rainforest.

I will give you
a golden box
from an Egyptian tomb.

I will give you
the shells of Crete.
...

I will give you
the feeling of a brown bear's skin.
and the sweetest sugar cane
on a barn field

I will give you
the beating drum in the moonlight
because I love you.
Jonathan (10)

This poem was written by a boy about a girl in the class who, he said, was his girl-friend. Compared to my generation, he expressed great honesty, reading his poem without snickering in an official, semi-public setting, his classroom, and using words of a tenderness associated with later years.

Other children, using the same structure 'I will give you' (more of this structure notion later) wrote:

> I will give you …
>
> the thread from a rainbow
> to sew in your memory
> After the rain has been falling …
> Laura (11)

'To sew in your memory' was added after I had asked, 'What use would that thread be? What could you do with it?' These prompts helped the writer to extend an already beautiful image with an especially appropriate phrase. We should, as teachers, be more alert than we usually are to the pedagogic value of open-ended questions. They are even more teacherly if we do not know the answer ourselves. Then, asking them becomes an act of faith in the child-writer's ability to do better than we can. It is often useful to move quickly away from a child after asking such questions, suggesting that the true writer is always on her own in the search for original ideas.

> the sound of a harp
> strung by the slimmest finger
> on the middle string

This was written after some instruction about alliteration. From the same poem:

> I will give you
> an end to your favourite poem
> but this is to be no
> ordinary poem it shall be this poem
> at its end.
> Stacey (10)

This is an unusual thing in children's writing, a poem that refers to itself.
  Some poems hinted at real tragedies:

> I will give you
> my eyes to once more see the world properly

This reminded me of Edward Thomas's 'And You Helen' in which he said he would like to give his short-sighted wife, among other things, 'A clear eye as good as mine'.
  Some writers displayed knowledge from other subjects: Danielle (11) offered to give someone 'the love from Aphrodite's temple'. Others spoke volumes about relationships with siblings:

If I could give my brother anything
I know what it would be.
A life without sadness, hurt or sorrow,
a place where he is free.

I would give him a garden with scents and sounds
and colours everywhere
and a good education
where teachers are always fair.

And peace to be always in his heart
and the sun to be his light,
for others to always care for him
and to be in a world that's bright.

I would give you
Jonathan my brother
happiness and peace from the Lord,
a smell of nature and glorious food
when you are sad.

I would give you
sounds that you love when you play.

I would give you
a good heart to be known popular throughout the nations.

I would help you to become
a full Christian
to help your family members
to have a useful job and a happy life.

I would give you
Jonathan my brother
love, joy, happiness and peace from the Lord
and a stream, and a forest, and animals.

Anon (12)

6 Lists

I have been hinting at the power of lists for some pages. Here is the idea at its most raw:

Things I like

Pretty girls
flying doves
lovely poems
bold men
fizzy drinks
summer holidays
and
lots of friends
> Jade (9)

I remember the writer of this poem well. She was on a course for children who wanted to be writers, but after a day and a half she had produced almost nothing that she or I were pleased with. She was not a fluent writer, and had been taught somehow or other that mechanical issues in language were all-important. So she was frightened of making mistakes. After a few false starts which distressed us both, I asked her simply to make a list of 'things she liked', and she came up with this little poem. It delighted her, and pleased me and the other children. I extended this idea by asking other children to write lists about things that they like, but leaving alternate lines blank. Then I ask them to fill in the empty lines with clauses beginning 'because ... ':

Things I like

Horses running
because they are fast.

Maths
because of the sums

My bunny
because of the hopping

Smells of Scottish air
because I come from Scotland.

Making things
because it is gluey.

Louise (8)

This next writer did not get far enough to write more than one of the 'because' lines because she kept rubbing out mistakes in her spelling ('arciologiy' for example). She, too, had been taught that accuracy in these mechanical issues was more important than the expression of her feelings, that getting secretarial details conventionally correct was more important than the formation of a shapely poem. Despite these pressures, her poem was so truthful, I print it as she left it (though I can't reproduce the bits of eraser and smudge all over it):

Things I like

Archaeology, the kind that's digging
because it is so interesting
the smell of jasmine
the taste of strawberry
swimming in warm water
sewing soft toys
when I am almost asleep
codling [*sic*] mummy and daddy

Anna (7)

I like sparkling glitter
because it is cool.
The softness of fur
because it is cuddly.
The taste of sour strawberry
because it is mouthwatering
gigantic soft toys
because they are warm

Natasha (7)

One writer, Nellie (7), was a traveller, and had spent only a few days in the school. She dictated her list to the headteacher, and among other elements in it was 'watching my grandad get better'.

I have already mentioned lists, because the gift poems in Chapter 5 are variations on this idea, and so are other ideas that I have described. The idea of the list may seem low-key to most of us. But it is a notion that many poets have used, and on which good poems have thrived. Rupert Brooke's poem 'The Great Lover' is another good example. It begins like this:

> I have been so great a lover: filled my days
> So proudly with the splendour of love's praise …

I always read these two lines in a big old-fashioned phony 'poetic' voice and ask the children to guess what the poem will be about. Of course they say 'his girlfriend(s)', 'his wife' etc. What happens is a good lesson for all of us; that love is there in the minutiae of life; 'Who sweeps a room, as for Thy laws, / Makes that and th'action fine'. After a few poor fag-end romantic lines, Brooke suddenly seems to find the required tone:

> These I have loved:
>   White plates and cups, clean-gleaming,
> Ringed with blue lines; and feathery, faery dust;
> Wet roofs, beneath the lamplight; the strong crust
> Of friendly bread; and many-tasting food;
> Rainbows; and the blue bitter smoke of wood;
> And radiant raindrops couching in cool flowers …
> Then, the cool kindliness of sheets, that soon
> Smooth away trouble; and the rough male kiss
> Of blankets; grainy wood; live hair that is
> Shining and free; blue-massing clouds; the keen
> Unpassioned beauty of a great machine;
> The benison of hot water; furs to touch;
> The good smell of old clothes; and others such –
> The comfortable smell of friendly fingers,
> Hair's fragrance, and the musty reek that lingers
> About dead leaves and last year's ferns …

It is as well to read as much as possible of the poem as will hold the class's attention, because the effect depends to a large extent on its accumulation of disparate objects, and their odd, unexpected juxtaposition: clouds, a great machine, fingers, hair, hot water. I point out to the children that Brooke uses all the senses: you can see, hear, smell, feel and taste the objects in the lines of his poem. You could also play the record of the song 'My Favourite Things' from *The Sound of Music*. I have never done this. This lyric rips off and sentimentalizes Brooke's idea, with its whiskers on kittens and so on. But it will add to the mix:

> These I have loved:
> a clock rattles and ticks on my bedside table.
> The sound of birds singing in the morning
> and the smell of a bonfire in autumn.
> The comfort of my bed and bedroom and
> also the friendly voice of my Mum.
> The smell of warm chocolate warms my heart

and the sound of a fire crackling by my side
and the warmth of my house gives me courage.
The taste of fresh crisp pizza
and the smell of chocolate pudding

I treasure all of these but most of all
I love my Mum and Dad.

Matthew (9)

These I have loved
The sound of raindrops on a metal roof,
the crunch of the snow when it is walked on,
the feel of a fresh breeze on a hot day,
the light of the moon coming through my window,
the crackle of an open fire,
the smell of a flower bud just opened,
the sound of the waves crashing against the rocks,
the smell of freshly baked cake,
the look of the stars glistening,
tasting hot chocolate after a cold day out,
smelling fresh chips straight from the oven.

Hannah (11)

These I have hated
A mess on the floor,
a nail being cut,
the sound of teachers' nails on the blackboard,
baked beans and melted chocolate,
dead trees and plants,
weeds as well.
I hate the smell of gone-off cheese
and to feel lumpy concrete with my knees.
Losing a friend can be bad too.
I hate to smell stinky breaths and smelly feet.
When I've washed my hands it gives me a little tingle up my back.
I hate the sight of spiders or any creepy-crawlies.
Like my brother.

Vanessa (10)

These I have hated

The smell of charcoal
    in a burnt out fire.

The texture of hot custard
    on a cold day.

Taste of milk
   other than with in tea or with cereal.

People cheering at Arsenal
   on television.

The uncooked texture
   and taste of potato.

People shouting at each other
   in argument.

The wail of the wind
   on a cold night.

                  David (9)

The technique of the class poem

I asked some infants to tell me sounds they loved, and the teacher wrote the list out as a poem:

I love to hear bees buzzing
and dolphins singing in the sea.
I love to hear
bells ringing in the church tower.
I love cats walking around the house.
I love to hear sugar pouring into bowls, I don't know why.
I love to hear cows mooing.
I love to hear babies crying in the cot.
I love to hear the kettle hum in the kitchen.
I love to hear the sound of the sea like a snake.
I love to hear the rain splashing on the road
I love the sound of it raining
and my brother Ross
laughing when my Mummy tickles him.

I love to hear
churches making a big noise in the night,
people clicking with their fingers.
I love to hear
the sound of biscuits crunching.

I love to hear
glass smashing
like stars twinkling
and the sound when people tread in the snow.

On a perfect Saturday morning ...

I wrote this next poem as an illustration of two techniques: listing and alliteration. The first technique, as I have shown, is a relatively simple matter. Everyone can list, and listing, unlikely as it seems, is a beginning of poetry. The second technique, even though it is used for subtle reasons by poets and novelists and, for less subtle reasons (MODEL MUDDLE MAKES MINISTER BLUSH) by journalists, does not present many problems in the teaching of it. As far as child-writers are concerned, alliteration is a useful introduction to a part of the music of poetry; to the fact that poetry doesn't just mean things, but also sings. Here, then, is a simple verse introduction to alliteration:

Things to do on the first day of the summer holidays

Lie in bed late, lounging and lolling about.
Eat eggs and bacon for breakfast at eleven.

Sprawl on the lawn with a long glass of lemonade
And eat salad and seafood. Travel the town, T-shirted,

Greeting mates, grinning with freedom. Bowl.
Bash those bails down. Belt a leather ball

Bouncing to the boundary, bounce, bounce ... Bring
A take-away home: parathas and pappadums.

Talk about treats: sunlight through trees, and sand.
Sleep in deep silence between sheets. Dream.

These poems were written by young writers on courses who have played with three things: my poem, the idea of lists and alliteration:

Snooze silently until the starlings start.
Play pinball powerfully.
Read restfully about the Romans.
Watch talking t.v. presenters.
Play ball blissfully, being careful not
To damage anything.
Dance daringly down the road.
Go shopping skidding skilfully down the aisles.
                                        Christopher (10)

Things to do on a perfect Sunday morning

Play football on a perfect pitch,
Climb bare, brown branches.
Play my tunes on my tuba.
Hop down to the Harlequin Centre.

Play in a tennis tournament.
Walk in wonderful woods
while collecting conkers.

                    Mark (9)

Endings

This list idea is a simple one again based on a repeated structure. I am going to write very little about this: indeed, I only worked on the idea because, for one reason or another, people asked me for work on endings. But now, when I look at this next poem, I reflect on how it is possible to use any remotely resonant phrase to get children writing.

And when I was asked for an idea about endings, the idea found a ready place in my mind. I remember when I was an adolescent that songs with the words 'over' in them had a peculiar piquancy. Roy Orbison's soaring, sloppy, vibrato-less tenor comes to mind singing 'It's over ... '. So does a Cliff Richard song with a similar title. Big weepies from Gene Pitney and others niggle at the edge of my mind as I write. I think all that attention on these songs was behind the use of this line, however it was disapproved of by elders and betters and, indeed, secretly, by myself.

But children have a happy way of using an idea, and, at the same time, consciously or not, deflating it:

Endings

When summer is over
I am as unhappy
as a baked bean
about to be eaten.

When the day is over
I am as happy as a horse
that has just won a race.

When the term is over
I am as relieved
as a toddler going to the toilet.

When the weekend is over
I am as angry
as a swatted fly.

When music is over
I am as calm
as a calm tree
on a calm day.

When a piece of music is over
I'm tempted like a thief
to play it again.

Tom (10)

Things they say and do

This lesson is another less emotionally charged variation on the lists theme (or more correctly, I suppose, the lists methodology). With young children (the examples here come from five- and six-year-olds) lists have the effect of delaying the mystification of poetry. Young children have no problem associating real life – play, pain, love, anger, pleasure – with this art that so baffles most adults, and that reminds those adults of a life that isn't real; a life that is, they sense obscurely, the life of another world; an art that involves mystifying language; an art that involves no play, no pain, no love, no anger, no pleasure; an art, though, that does use that queer thing, rhyme, and words that are not in general use in the fish shop, or the pub, or at the Henley Regatta, or in the House of Commons; or anywhere normal people meet.

Delay that mystification! Poetry uses all words, and does not need to be mysterious. Lists are useful in teaching this. For a start, in lists there is rarely much chance for rhyme, and also the subject matter is resolutely everyday. Lists also demonstrate that everyone can contribute something. **Poetry is a democratic subject: it is not just for God's golden children.** I ask the children to close their eyes and think of things that 'teachers often say to them'. An adult writes down the remarks that they offer, after I've asked the teacher (this is said to be overheard by the children) that s/he is not to use his or her 'best writing', or to bother about rubbing anything out; that s/he will have to be quick, or s/he will miss good things and that s/he must 'scribble', or 'jot' things down. This is part of another general principle: **the secretarial and the compositional** have to be distinguished. Making things and neatness are not necessarily connected. Indeed, creativity will usually involve untidiness, because there is an essential urge to make order; and chaos is a prerequisite of order. Later, the teacher puts all the sayings separately on cards, and the children arrange them in an appropriate order. The children are learning about their teachers and their relationship with their teachers; they are learning about school and its nature; they are learning in groups about what things go best with what; and they are learning, to some real purpose, words that matter – their own words.

Things that teachers always say

Time for the register
Do your work.
Don't bother to get a rubber, just leave your work like that.
Hold your pencil properly.

Tidy up your table.
Line up quickly.
Before your dinner you have to wash your hands.

Reception class

Go in the quiet room.
Watch the television quietly.
Don't run in school, you have to walk.
Sit down properly.
Cross your legs.
Be quiet.
Get a book to read.
Go outside.
Go on the field.
Don't be scared.
Get the pencils please.
Don't scribble.
That's good writing.
Well done.
Put the pencils away.

Year 1 class

Would it perhaps be embarrassing for us as teachers to reflect, however briefly, on these lists? The picture that emerges of the school is of an institution more like the army than anything else, where orders are given and obeyed, and where even recreation (we might call it 'exercise time') is dictated to the children: 'Go outside. Go on the field'. In this connection, I reflect how children are lined up at the end of each break, and more or less marched in 'without talking, please' at the blast of a whistle, or a peremptory shout. I don't know whether, in the army, or in prison, there are clear instructions given and daily insisted on about how soldiers and prisoners should sit, but we can see from these lines that children are given such instructions many times a day. It is interesting here that no words are remembered that could be considered undoubtedly about learning: the words are administrative, disciplinary and managerial, but never educational.

What do parents say?

Put your socks on.
Put your shoes on the right feet.
Don't be late for school.
Brush your hair.
Put your hairclips in.
Don't mess about.
Don't cry.
Don't be silly.
Have your breakfast.

Obsessions

This is work built on children's own obsessions, from toys and hobbies to advanced intellectual, artistic and scientific pursuits. We tap these obsessions all too rarely when we teach children to write. Although children have the subjects for their poems in their daily lives – horse riding, fishing, sailing, dancing, pop music, science, zoology – we as teachers usually ignore such material in favour of what is stamped with the words NATIONAL CURRICULUM. We are afraid that giving too much to children in the way of subject matter in writing will give them control, and, by the same token, take some of ours away. Or, more particularly, we are frightened that politicians and inspectors will see us as leaking power from their centre: Millbank, or the Department of this or that. Take too much of their power away.

All intellectually healthy and inquisitive humans have obsessions. Work on children's obsessions frees them to deepen their awareness of all kinds of phenomena. As a motor mechanic, my late friend Robin traded in words like 'camshaft', 'carburettor' and 'air cooler' – all more or less incomprehensible to me – and collected and read, for pleasure as well as for work, repair manuals. A human's obsessions are often dismissed as jargon, 'as though every passion does not have its lexicon' (Sedgwick in Styles *et al* 1994:200)

I asked this next writer what her obsession was, and whether she could make a quick brainstormed list of words concerned with that obsession. We sorted the words into groups: nouns, verbs and adjectives, and slowly, over an hour or so, she made this draft of a poem:

> Eyepins, earclips, shiny, new
> beads are my favourite,
> rose red, grass green, any colour will do.
> Bugles come in any shade but only one shape.
> They're tiny, fiddly, hard to handle and small.
>
> Eyepins, earclips, shiny, new.
> Christmas is the best time to buy
> when all the clips are cheap
> and in the shops there's unusual beads
> with glistery streaks.
>
> I adore to see the beads spread out
> like leaves in fall,
> I thread beads on to the wire.
> Eyepins, earclips, shiny, new,
> turquoise, magenta, any colour will do.
>
> I must have satisfaction before I clip off the wire.
> Bending the wire is the hardest bit.
> The long-nose pliers are made of metal
> and they're greasy in the middle.
> My hands are hot and sweaty

trying to get the loop just right.

Eyepins, earclips, shiny, new,
blues and yellows, any colour will do.

Improving self-esteem in an Essex primary school: three ideas
(with acknowledgements to Sophie Chipperfield)

There is in me

My friend Sophie Chipperfield sent me these poems. I don't know much about how she taught them, except that she got the idea from children's writing published elsewhere. So the roundabout of ideas goes on, as ways of getting children to write, change and grow in the hands of enthusiastic teachers. Although I was not present, I can infer much of the lesson from the poems, as can the reader. It is a powerful way of writing seriously about oneself. Sophie wrote to me:

> I feel that this writing is all about the children's trust and honesty with themselves and with me: having the strength to write down such personal expressions of personality. I love the fact that they are all so different, and the children loved the fact that I could tell whose poem was whose having read them only once or twice.

There is in me
a cat on
the wall purring.

There is in me
a mental maniac
running up and down the stairs.

There is in me
a hamster running
in its wheel all day.

There is in me
the moon shining in the street.

There is in me
a lizard hissing
in his tank.

There is in me
a number being
counted.

Thomas (8)

There is in me
the army
out doing training.

There is in me
a pencil
drawing on its own.

There is in me
my mum and dad
fighting.

There is in me
a friend
being naughty.

There is in me
a fat snake
getting squashed.

There is in me
a war that will never end.

                              Jason (8)

There is in me
A white hamster
Quiet and shy.

There is in me
A small black spider
Tiptoeing through my heart.

There is in me
A rude lion
Yawning in the grass.

There is in me
A brain
Working faster than a steam train.

There is in me
A big red heart with lots of love.

There is in me
A tiny green tree
Lost in the middle of nowhere.

                              Donna (9)

Sophie has written on this the comment 'a child with considerable difficulties, emotional and academic. A moving piece of writing, very Donna'.

This next exercise from Sophie Chipperfield is similar. It is simple enough. Collect words about feelings ('sad', 'confident', 'happy', 'surprised', 'excited' etc.) and then ask the children to use them in a list as Thomas does in the first poem.

> I was sad my Nan died.
> I was sad my Nanna was dead.
> I was sad my home got burnt down.
> I was sad I didn't have any friends.
> I was sad I missed my Nanna.
> I was sad my Grandad was dead.
> I was sad my Nanna has gone away.
> I was sad I had no person.
> I was sad I missed my Nanny.
> I was sad I got kicked.
>
> Thomas (6)

A simple exercise, I said. But look at Thomas's obsessive repetition of his Nanny's name. Here the learning to be celebrated is about the writer's emotions, and who can question that it is intense, and, whether it is measurable or not, expressed with an honesty most adult writers could not aspire to. It seems to me that here is an example of a child writing about deep misery; facing up to it bravely, paying attention to it and learning about it, as if he, somehow, knew that 'for every effort of attention … a light that is in exact proportion to [it] will one day flood the soul' (Simone Weil in Panichas 1977). This next writer is paying attention to more positive aspects of her experience and character:

> I was confident
> I was confident
> to read my lovely poem I was confident
> to read a sparkling book I was confident
> to ride my bike I was confident
> to play basketball I was confident
> to help my friend I was confident
> to take a shower I was confident
> to sing a lovely song I was confident
> to write a story I was confident
> to say a prayer I was confident
> to count to one hundred
>
> Anon (6)

I felt, as soon as I saw this writing, that its odd format may or may not have been arrived at by chance; but I also felt that, either way, all writers need luck occasionally, and this had a pleasingly strange shape that was worth preserving.

The next piece had an obscurity in the first line, which I liked. After all, modern poetry is notoriously obscure – why shouldn't examples of it written by children be that way too? Also, I liked the way the relatively trivial – the T-shirt and the PlayStation – jostled for position with growing up. Note, too, the appearance of that bureaucratic nonsense, the level, in children's writing:

> I was surprised I went to Flamingo Lunch.
> I was surprised I got a Sunderland T-shirt.
> I was surprised I grew up.
> I was surprised it was the end of school.
> I was surprised I passed the hardest level.
> I was surprised it was winter.
> I was surprised it was night, and I could get my telescope out.
> I was surprised to get a PlayStation.
>
> David (7)

Finally from this Essex school, Sophie Chipperfield seems to specialize in work that helps children to write about their potential:

> I am a dull piece of metal,
> Make me the flashy robot.
> I am a fluffy duck,
> Make me the golden eagle.
>
> Jesse (9)

> I am a tiny minnow,
> Make me the giant pike.
> I am a young boy,
> Make me the handsome prince.
> I am a dislodged brick,
> Make me the Great Wall of China.
> I am a small stone,
> Make me the steep cliff.
> I am a fluffy little cat,
> Make me the king of the jungle.
>
> James (9)

> I am a melted chocolate
> Make me the Cadbury castle.
> I am a worthless boy,
> Make me the strongest god.
>
> Matthew (9)

> I am a tin of vegetables,
> Make me a gravy roast.
> I am a flame,
> Make me the blazing sun.

I am the first number,
Count me to infinity.
                    Michaela (10)

Mirror lists

This lesson depends on some thinking and talk about mirrors. Questions and stimuli like this help:

What are mirrors for?

Can you think of different kinds of mirrors? (Corbett and Moses 1986, where I first came across this idea, list as examples shop windows, reflections from water and eyes, as well as looking-glasses)

What would you see in a mirror if you could see your past?

Your future?

Let the conversation go into the abstract:

Can a mirror lie?

Can we hide from mirrors?

My friend Julie Taplin read the children Sylvia Plath's poem 'Mirror', quoted in Corbett and Moses, and found in her *Collected Poems* (1981:173). The children wrote:

I wake up.
A Neanderthal man looks at me.
He is puzzled, he has never seen himself before.
Now someone in royal robes puts a sword in a stone.
I reflected him faithfully.
Now some teenagers are drinking beer.
They throw their cans at me.
Once I was clear but now I am murky.
With shopping trolleys and rubbish
I am like a rubbish dump.
Industry waste oozes from pipes into me
Filling me to the brim.
                    Anon (11)

The funfair mirror
Is inexact,
Curved, cruel, cuddly
Like jelly wobbling …
                    Lauren (11)

... I lie.
A pretty girl looks at me,
A wailing elephant of a girl stares back!
I just calmly stand
Like a stiff stony statue
Wishing I could join her world.

Alice (10)

I am a tired mirror
Closed in a gloomy bag,
The slave of a young girl
Reflecting her appearance.
Every hour she wakes me
And she snatches me
From my dreams.
She dresses her lips with ruby red
Then looks at me in disgust.
Quickly replaced
I am stuck once more
With scented perfume and powder
Which makes me sneeze.

Hannah (10)

A girl needs me
I reflect truthful what I see.
She searches my depths for her beauty,
Her long brown hair shining ...
She tosses her head and walks away
Proud of what she sees.
Many years passed.
She returns to the mirror.

The reflection which was once beautiful
Is now hit by age,
Grey, old and wrinkly!

Grace (10)

Elegies: Children writing about death

Thomas's poem (see p.102) is like an elegy for his Nanna. In fact, the elegy is a genre that children enjoy using. It is a powerful genre, too, because it involves thinking about death and loss – of animals first, then of human beings. This one was written by an eleven-year-old boy whose father had died a year before. Obviously the song 'Fear no more the heat o' the sun' in *Cymbeline* inspires it. For more examples of the use of these lines, see my 1999c book. But, even more importantly, it shows the power poetry has to help children to write about the worst terrors of their lives:

> Fear no more
> The car's been sold.
> Fear no more
> Of making your bed
> And mending my bat.
> Fear no more
> Of the work you've done.
> Fear no more
> The farm's still standing
> And your bed's not bloodstained.
> Fear no more
> Your grave is done.

Birth and death are two dangerous, important subjects. They are the big guns, along with love, in the poet's armoury. Because they are so serious, it is important that children write about them. Too often we avoid these subjects, especially death. It is not possible, obviously, to set up good lessons for either of these subjects. That would be, I think, improper, even indecent. But it is possible to be on the alert for when a young writer needs to write about either of them. If I had a classroom now, there would be in it a writing corner. On it would be at least the following:

- paper of different sizes, shapes and colours,
- forms (while adults hate filling in these, children love it),
- pads for messages and the like,
- an old typewriter,
- a computer with a word processor program in it,
- markers: pencils, felt-tips, ballpoints, crayons,
- office accessories: hole punches, rulers, old diaries.

This area would always be open for children who needed to celebrate the birth of a friend's baby:

> Your skin is wrinkly
> and soft as new cotton wool.
> You moan and whinge for food.
> Your mother watches you
> pass between visitors.
> She has a permanent loving smile.
> Fondly she kisses your forehead.
> You look up to her and yawn.

Your father holds you
firmly and carefully
as he would
a delicate,
fragile egg.
He is thinking
'This is what we've waited for'.
Your hiccuping little squeaks
shake your whole body.
Visitors laugh.
You, not sharing the joke,
hiccup again
and look annoyed.

                    Daniel (12)

This corner would also be there for young writers who were ready to mourn a death:

I saw in her eyes
a smile
I was sure she was
trying her best
her right hand puffed
out of size
her right hand was dead
her left hand
gripped my right.
And at that moment
I saw what she had
been trying to do
a huge toothy grin
her teeth were out of line.
It was one of the happiest
moments of my life
but it was one of the saddest
17 days later she died.

                    Daniel (12)

The writing corner where both of these poems were written was in the writer's bedroom. Thank God it was there. What if there is no writing corner at school, and still babies are born and old people – and young people – die? Where will the writer write? Where will s/he learn through the medium of words about the biggest events that happen? Where will s/he begin to come to terms with love, and death and grief?

Very late in my making of this book, a child wrote this next piece. She had been inspired by Angela Topping's poem referred to on p.84. The child has learnt as she wrote about herself and her relationship with her grandfather, about her relationships with her sisters and her sisters' relationship with the grandfather that they never knew. It is our responsibility, as teachers, to learn what we can from work like this. At the lowest level, we won't dismiss it. At the highest, we will examine it, and trust that the children who write for us in our classrooms have something important to teach us. We will then try to learn from them:

> He was my best mate
> before he went to Heaven.
>
> He called me EmmaLoo.
> We played together inside
> and outside.
>
> He was very good at
> making things.
>
> He was a coalman.
> My sisters never saw him.
> I feel sorry for them.
> He was my grandad.
>
> Emma (8)

Part III

Putting art in prison to set it free

7 Pattern

Pattern is there in all art. Look, for example, at the arches of a cathedral. Repeated shapes, seen from the west door along the nave to the choir, and further into the sanctuary, take our eyes down the length of the building with their leaping and sinking rhythm. Along the way we see other patterns: high up, the clerestory, and below that, smaller arches and twirls around huge pillars; stained glass windows with their repeated arched points, and variations of biblical stories. Pattern is in the music that I've just turned off to draft this. It's jazz, and the drum and bass rhythm keeps the complex pattern going as the trumpet flares, like a freed prisoner, above them. Suddenly the tenor sax mutters, preparing a solo ... That trumpet, that tenor, though ... neither of them is really free. Each instrument's player has his or her patterns: little flames of melody that soar from a note and return to it. These patterns both imprison the player and set him free.

Pattern is there in painting and drawing. This is especially present, but not only, in abstract art, where the pattern may be (apparently) random (Jackson Pollock) or extremely measured (Mondrian). Pattern dominates in the African fabrics around the walls of my dining room: little repeated human figures stand in rows and columns, each one lightly distinguished from its neighbour. To take an obvious example of figurative art, look at Van Gogh's *Sunflowers*. There is a repeated pattern in each orange circle. The concentric circles rhyme with each other. The green leaves echo with the orange leaves, and the table top's yellow is picked out in the flowers. A study of the picture in reproduction will bring out other patterns. Let's look until it hurts.

So pattern restricts art. I need that quotation again: 'Art has to be put into a prison in order to be set free'. I cannot write about Love or Death (my emotions about them are easy and valueless) but I can write about my love for my son, and the death of my father and mother: those emotions are locked in relationships and, more especially, for the purpose of art, in memories. These emotions do not require capital letters. They are particular and trapped. People and my feelings about them represent cells in which I write about love and death in general: Love and Death.

Now, I could imprison my feelings, and writing, even more by using poetic forms: little couplets for example, or haiku, or poems consisting of a certain number of syllables (see Sedgwick 2000 a, b and c). Locking feelings in patterns sets them free. It might be a contradiction or, if I am lucky, a paradox, but I might find that my feelings are even more expressed (from the Latin, pressed out) under the constraints of those forms. This part of my book is about various confinements and prison cells: rhyme, repeating lines, alliteration and repetition. Understanding of parts of all these techniques will help young writers to appreciate the subtle elements of pattern that we see and hear and feel in rhythm. First of all in cumulative poems like my own 'The ring lay on the desk' and 'I am the cat' (1994a) and traditional rhymes like 'One man went to mow'.

Cumulative poems

There is a pattern-tradition in English folk poetry: the poem that grows as the writer (or, more likely, the anonymous oral source) repeats each line, and adds another each time. Most people know about the old lady who swallowed a fly and ended up eating a horse 'to catch the cow ... to catch the dog ... to catch the cat ... to catch the bird ... to catch the spider (that wriggled and tickled inside her) ... to catch the fly'. Most people know, too, about the man who went to mow a meadow on his own, and ended up with a company of helpers; or about the old woman who bought a pig 'But pig would not go'; she employs a succession of animals and other natural forces to make the pig go – dog, stick, fire, water, ox, butcher, rope, rat and cat. Children love these rhymes. They relish the patterns, the growing anarchy, and the verbal energy of such pieces. And so do I.

I am not reprinting any of these rhymes here because they are readily available – first in the memories of many teachers and children, and second in anthologies such as the Opies' *Oxford Nursery Rhyme Book*. They are useful for getting young children – say between five and seven – writing group poems. This activity serves three aspects of the literacy hour, if not more. There is the writing, the plenary sessions and, underrated in my view, the reading in a subsequent hour. This activity offers three benefits for children's reading. They have repetition, and the resultant reinforcement of certain words, sounds and phrases; the words are the children's own: they literally own them, and the subject matter will therefore interest them; and, finally, the pattern element adds excitement and a mixture of predictability and unpredictability (will there be a slight change at any point?)

> The marmalade cat snores.
> The marmalade cat snores on the unmade bed.
> The marmalade cat snores on the unmade bed and the boy's bedroom is
>   silent and covered in clothes and comics.
> The marmalade cat snores on the unmade bed and the boy's bedroom is
>   silent and covered in clothes and comics. Outside a purple bush sways
>   in the light wind.
> The marmalade cat snores on the unmade bed and the boy's bedroom is
>   silent and covered in clothes and comics. Outside a purple bush sways
>   in the light wind. Still the writer sits at the desk.
> The marmalade cat snores on the unmade bed and the boy's bedroom is
>   silent and covered in clothes and comics. Outside a purple bush sways

in the light wind. Still the writer sits at the desk, and clouds move faster than his imagination.

The marmalade cat snores on the unmade bed ...

As you can see, these pieces are not hard to construct, and they are verses made for computers in their cut and paste role! I would suggest that you try making one up yourself. 'At the supermarket I chose burgers for John. / At the supermarket I chose burgers for John and a spiky pineapple for me' and so on. Children are usually impressed when told a new work is by their teacher.

On one occasion, the teacher divided the class into groups of five children each, making sure that there was a fluent scribe in each group. This exercise also involves negotiation, and teaches children to be tolerant of each other's views and also to be flexible. Both of these are qualities that are going to be crucial in a changing world. It is odd when this flexibility is not encouraged in successive government pronouncements, when skills that will have passed their sell-by date by the time the children hit what ministers call 'the job market' – mental arithmetic, keyboard skills on old computers, perfect conventional spelling and punctuation – are valued by them.

The class had recently visited Orford Castle in Suffolk, and one group was sitting under a display they had made with their teacher about their trip: pictures of the castle, books about castles, an Ordnance Survey map and books about Suffolk in the past. On the wall there were also some drawings by the children done at the castle, and some notes written there:

> I know a castle.
> I know a castle that's down the road.
> I know a castle that's down the road, that's as big as an elephant.
> I know a castle that's down the road that's as big as an elephant. It's called Orford Castle.
> I know a castle that's down the road that's as big as an elephant. It's called Orford Castle and it has a drawbridge.
> I know a castle that's down the road that's as big as an elephant. It's called Orford Castle and it has a drawbridge and it is the oldest.
> I know a castle that's down the road that's as big as an elephant. It's called Orford Castle and it has a drawbridge and it is the oldest and it had a portcullis.
> I know a castle that's down the road that's as big as an elephant. It's called Orford Castle and it has a drawbridge and it is the oldest and it had a portcullis and a tower.
> It has collapsed.

Another group used the local park:

> I know a park.
> I know a park with a swing.
> I know a park with a swing and a slide.

> I know a park with a swing and a slide and a circus.
> I know a park with a swing and a slide and a circus and a duckpond with
> people feeding ducks.
> I know a park with a swing and a slide and a circus and a duckpond with
> people feeding ducks and a mansion with a play area.
> I know a park with a swing and a slide and a circus and a duckpond with
> people feeding ducks and a mansion with a play area and lots of people.
> I know a park with a swing and a slide and a circus and a duckpond with
> people feeding ducks and a mansion with a play area and lots of people
> and a doll's house.
> I know a park with a swing and a slide and a circus and a duckpond with
> people feeding ducks and a mansion with a play area and lots of people
> and a doll's house and in the doll's house there are

'It ends like that because there is a mystery' said the leader of the group that wrote this, though the teacher and I felt that she was making a virtue of necessity, and that the group had simply run out of time (but not ideas).

Syllabic patterns

One way of introducing junior children to the notion of pattern in poetry is to teach them about syllables. The first thing I do is to play with names: I point out that Jenny's, for example, has two syllables, Martin's has two, as well; Rahima's has three. I go further, simply by introducing surnames: Jenny Taylor has four syllables in her name, Martin Benson-White five in his, and Rahima Begum has five in her name, as well. After some initial coaching, the work in this section presents few problems.

Haiku are something of a cliché. Everyone who has approached the beginnings of teaching poetry to juniors has had a go at them. But they are still useful – far more useful, it might as well be said, than acrostics, that random structure that offers nothing to either learning or poetry (insofar as the two things can be distinguished). Haiku have five syllables in the first of their three lines, seven in the second, and five in the third. They normally focus on some natural phenomenon, and comment, as implicitly as possible, on it. Stillman (1966) writes that:

> No consideration of meter or rhyme enters into the technique of such a poem – only the rather stark progression of syllables adding up to an image that implies far more than it says …

In their insistence on concentration on language, the component parts of a word, they make the writer study the phenomenon being examined (sea, mirror, cat) too:

> Waves on the shore. They
> live out at sea. Explode, roll
> and die with a hiss.
>
> John (12)

Here is my face: still
a child's, my hair like oil. One
    day, silver will come.
                          Farida (10)

My cat Norman
    Across two gardens
he scuttles to me when I
    call his silly name.
                          Ann (11)

Tanka are haiku with two extra lines of seven syllables each:

In the night I hear
a silence where my old dog
    used to bark. I wish
he was there to annoy us
all now! But there's only silence.
                          Jeremy (12)

A cinquain (invented, children are always delighted to learn, by one Adelaide Crapsey) contains two syllables in the first line, four in the second, six in the third, eight in the fourth and two in the last:

This day
or this cold night
I hear crunching snow
under my feet and fast car tyres
skidding.
                          Nicola (10)

In the
dark house I sit
waiting for the sunrise
and for the new-born birds to sing.
Waiting.
                          Joe (9)

Children can invent their own syllabic stanza, as I have in this poem, which is about the death of a footballer on the pitch during a game. It is written in stanzas that are composed of, respectively, four, four, six, seven and nine syllable lines. I find counting syllables takes some of the heat out of subjects like death:

Match abandoned

>   That day was not
>   the day sun shone
>   or we stood swallowing
>   beer in the pub garden, but
> the day you, imperfect stranger, died.
>
>   Stripped to football's
>   heraldry, you
>   gulped the tip of your tongue,
>   writhed, and to the lads all was
> slow-motion, video-vivid.
>
>   Distant friend,
>   statistic ungraced
>   with Hillsborough, Bradford,
>   or Heysel, you collapsed
> in the afternoon sun. The world stopped.
>
>   Small boys worried
>   to the parents.
>   Stretcher bearers swapped looks.
>   The crowd, four-square, hushed at
> one match no one could take as it came.
>
>   In this photo
>   you sit like a
>   good schoolboy, ready for
>   assembly, legs crossed, hands
> clasped, never to magnetize the crowd
>
>   to its feet again,
>   never to joke
>   in the communal bath,
>   or swear at referee,
> fullback; please from touchline for the ball.
>
>   I can understand
>   like everyone
>   no death. But yours, that caught
>   you in the centre of this
> appalled rectangle – Boys cry out of the ground
>
> hands once more in the fathers' hands.

I break my rules once or twice. But what are rules for? As long as you concentrate
hard on trying to obey them, they do their work.

Oxymorons

This section is based on the phrase 'brawling love' and other oxymorons from *Romeo and Juliet*. The word 'oxymoron' comes from the Greek, and means (as *SOED* says) 'a rhetorical figure by which contradictory terms are conjoined so as to give point to the statement or expression'. I have written at length about this in my 1999c book. What follows are oxymorons that have been written since that book was published. I have realized that the power of this exercise lies in a fact that seemed obvious once it had dawned on me: oxymorons are patterns that, for the time being, simply prevent the possibility of cliché. An oxymoron is a pattern that requires opposites.

I ask children, first, to listen to two speeches from *Romeo and Juliet* (1:1:167–73 and 3:2:73–79; in Sedgwick 1999c on pp.108–9). I read these lines, emphasizing the oxymorons, with a different voice for each half of each one. Then, 'What' I ask them 'is the main characteristic of these speeches?'. Someone always says that they're opposites or contrasts. I ask the children to invent oxymorons. This is difficult at first, but as soon as each child produces an example, however ordinary it is ('fat thin') for example, I praise it as much as I dare, and the encouragement inevitably leads to something more interesting. Here is a list that a class of ten-year-olds came up with:

> waterproof – sponge
> boiling – snow
> ice with friction
> freezing fire
> white – black
> transparent wood
> evil angel
> crawling humans
> opaque glass
> beautiful ugliness
> wet electricity
> dry water
> green sky

Once the children have grasped the idea, and realized that it isn't a very difficult matter, I ask them to take one of their oxymorons, and to extend it into a little three- or four-line poem – either by adding another oxymoronic phrase, or by linking it with another of their oxymorons. The very shortness of the poem required is an encouragement. And the good short poem has a collision of feeling and form inside it that makes it especially valuable:

An oxymoronic poem

Waterproof sponge
that shrinks to the size
of an elephant.

Wet electricity
that works
and doesn't glow.

Opaque glass
that you
can see through.

Devastating happiness
with joyous death.
                    Jenny (10)

Burning ice
that hurts
as it hovers
in mid-air.

Speedy sloth
as fast as a slug.

Bright blackness
that lights my way
through the pitch black forest.

Loving cruelty
that comforts me
when I am happy.

Precious rubbish
that is worth more
than a worthless pebble.
                    Joshua (10)

I referred above to 'a collision of feeling and form', but there is also an element of chance in this kind of writing; chance that children will discover and write about feelings with more than the usual form, because of lines that contradictory phrases and words will throw into their minds. All writers – all artists – need a little luck sometimes, and the luck, I have found, that comes when children are searching for contradictions, is often the most potent of all:

Strange familiarity
that helps me to know nothing
except what I remember forgetting.
                    Jerome (12)

Child teaches teacher:
This is what you must not do,
What I do.
                    D J (12)

8 Using visual images

Postcards

I wish now that I had never thrown any postcards away. Even views of beaches and landscapes, towns and stately homes and churches have their uses in reminding me of my past and my friends' pasts, and where I was and who I was with when I received (for example) this picture of a crowded beach at Blackpool, or that Lowry reproduction of an industrial Salford scene, or this smutty joke, postmarked, improbably, Frinton-on-Sea. After ten years or so, even postmarks and stamps become interesting. Every little part of each side of each card has all sorts of bizarre ramifications, some of them undreamt of when the card was chosen and written on, in some art gallery, or on some beach, or in some pub or café.

What about this one, received today? A pig looks forward, and a man holds up something, a truffle, I think, with a cheerful expression on his (the man's) face. A teacher of poetry could do worse than to collect all the postcards s/he receives, from wherever they arrive, and whatever they depict. You could make a poem from a one-line description of all the cards in a collection from a given year:

> On Armistice Night flags flew
> > soldiers sang
> Sunlight on Brownstones: a man
> > and a woman look into unnatural light
> A child with a bouquet of flowers
> > clutches a forgotten satchel
> Leather-skinned, Bear Bull Blackfoot
> > outstares the horizon
> At Abydos they magically re-enact
> > the sacred journey of Osiris ...

and so on

A friend of mine, Duncan Allan, specializes in writing inconsequential stories on his holiday postcards. The picture propped up against my monitor now one is of some ancient houses on the Greek island of Tilos, all irregular brick shapes and holes, and the occasional wooden door. Light and shade play their dramatic part:

the intensity of some dark parts, the intensity of the light everywhere else. I turn the card over. He writes:

> Have spent the last ¾ of an hour watching an ever increasing number of ants trying to make off with a portion of my shortbread biscuit – they are very determined. What they don't realize is that they won't be able to get it down their hole. I haven't the heart to tell them. John [Duncan's seventeen-year-old son] tells me that the Greek priests ought to be a little more catholic in their dress sense – 'What shall we wear tomorrow? Black. And the day after? Black'. Ooh it's so exciting … Some good doorways to be seen up in the old village – solid and simple but they really do the job. Choose your stone with care is, I think, the motto. Off to Halki on Wednesday. Hope the priests are ready for us …

I quote this in answer to many teachers who tell me that they cannot write. Don't try and be funny. Just tell it (as they used to say) like it is. Observe. Put it down.

I have kept many cards. The most valuable cards for the classroom are cards with art on them, preferably people, with their faces prominent. I save these in a shoebox. And I buy those bound collections of art cards that are to be had very cheaply in remainder shops in high streets in all the towns I know: shops with names like 'The Works' and 'Books Books Books', advertising books at bargain prices. I have not reproduced any of the pictures here, because of copyright and cost problems; in any case, it would better to use pictures from collections personally amassed.

The following work is by six- and seven-year-olds who had spent time examining part of my collection. The children had all the freedom that they felt they needed in choosing the kinds of things they might write. They could be:

- descriptions of the picture (emphasize colour and shape, and possible smells and sounds and tastes; emphasize details that might be missed on a first look, and that might only be seen after many stares – see my description below);
- what you might like to ask the people in the picture;
- what they might say to each other.

Children should also know that if they start with one kind of sentence, they can feel free to change to other kinds.

Here are two poems of my own, based on famous pictures that I have, unfortunately, seen only in reproduction. The original of the first is in Vienna, but there is an excellent reproduction in *The Art Book* (Phaidon 1994:71). First, I offer a prose description of a Bruegel painting, *Peasant Wedding Feast*. I offer these words partly in defence of my main principle, that of observation. How closely do we look at pictures?

> We look here at a bustling scene. It's nearly all beiges and browns, except for occasional splashes of red in jackets and caps, and neat touches of green on other clothing. We are in a room chock-full of peasant revellers drinking and eating, pouring wine or beer into jugs, carrying flat bowls, or plates, of soup, or pies, possibly, on a door that has been taken off its hinges; or playing bagpipes.

One of the pipers stares pathetically, hungrily at the food. A dog peers out from under a table, timeless, unlike the human beings, who are trapped in their century by their clothes. The bride sits, rather smug, it's hard not to feel, under a red and white striped object that, presumably, denotes her temporary status. It's obviously a symbol of some sort. Her eyes are closed, her hands rest piously together on her lap. 'Legend has it' my reference book tells me 'that Bruegel would put on disguises in order to take part in the peasants' rollicking gatherings'. Looking again at this reproduction, it's easy to believe in such authenticity. In the foreground, so close that you could reach out and tickle him or her, or pat the extravagantly hatted head, is a little person. It could be a girl or a boy. Whoever it is licks food off her fingers. S/he is the speaker in my poem:

Peasant Wedding Feast
(Pieter Bruegel the Elder)

Oh the noise! the clatter
of plates on tables, the songs,
the jokes, the laughter, the smells

of burning meat, of ale spilled, of
coarse wine –

I shuffle along
the floor at my auntie's wedding
and eat myself nearly sick.

I will snooze through the afternoon
in my father's arms, till I wake
to 'Show me the way to go home'
sung in Dutch by my Uncle Pieter.

The other picture has no human beings in it: it is *Café at Night* (Van Gogh):

OK.
What's going on here?

Under a cloth of sky
marked with stars and brush-strokes
and evergreen shutters and trees
there are tables like kettle-drums
and chairs on a brown rug
on the cobbled pavement.

What would you like to drink?

Have you anything like
that bright heaven colour
the gas lights throw on the wall?
I might never be thirsty again.

There are at least two ways in which we can use pictures like this. One is to get children to write straight descriptions of the pictures, as in my paragraph above. The children should have the instructions to make the mood of the writing as much like the picture as possible. I hope my paragraph, for example, with its long and short sentences mixed together, enacts the bustling character of the Bruegel. I hope I have conveyed some sense of the scene with simple description of colour, and with description of expressions of faces.

Looking intensively at pictures helps the children with their writing, of course. The material is almost palpable, and you don't have to search for a subject. Make an effort with a good picture, and all your sense can come into play, even smell. But such looking helps with Art as well. Once one has written about a picture (or a place, come to that) it becomes more one's own. This activity (we must say in our increasingly mechanistic times) serves the Art curriculum. It helps us to look at a world that deserves far more looking than it gets.

So children can write simple description. Children can also write a poem. This can be one of the following:

- a simple description of the picture;
- words addressed to someone or even something in the picture;
- words to be spoken by someone or something in the picture.

Daniel was looking at an etching of a couple at the seaside. The young man is staring morosely into the palm of his right hand, where there are three paltry-looking coins. The other hand is stuffed into his pocket, and his face wears an expression of extreme glumness. The young woman hugs herself again the cold, and looks expressionlessly away from both her man and the sea. The picture is called *We Weren't Going Anywhere*, and it is by John Duffin, and it was exhibited at the RAA summer exhibition in 1995. My friend Duncan (it was his message on the back of a card quoted above) has sent me messages on copies of this card more than once, and I associate it with him and his love of humour in modern figurative British art.

> Oh boy I've got 20p left.
> It's not enough for an ice cream.
> It's not enough for a drink.
> It's not enough for a new jacket
> 'cos this one is old and tacky.
>
> Oh hurry up, I'm freezing
>
> It's not enough for …
>
> Oh shut up!
> I'm bored of hearing you,
> It's not enough
>
> Daniel (7)

Anna had drawn from my pile of cards a painting by Chagall. *The Walk* is in the Hermitage Museum in St Petersburg, and shows a smart young man waving his maroon-dressed, rather uncertain-looking girl in the air.

> How can I fly in the sky?
> How can I hold you up?
> I am really light.
> You're really light.
> I'm wearing a beautiful dress, aren't I?
> Yes you are aren't you.
>
> The town is made of shapes,
> rectangles, triangles, cylinders.
> The big cathedral in the background stands out because it is pink.
>
> Anna (7)

Anna had finished at the end of the first section, and I suggested she said something about the background.

Edward Hopper

Four of the children found themselves looking at reproductions of enormous paintings by Edward Hopper. *Nighthawks* (1942) is in the Art Institute of Chicago and is probably his most famous picture. It shows a massive gloomy bar with three customers and a barman; the whole room is bathed in a typical, slightly eerie light. *Sunlight on Brownstones* (1956) from the Wichita Art Museum shows a couple at the front door of a house; again the light, though natural this time, has a worrying, electrical feel to it. *Chop Suey* (1929, from a private collection) shows two women, capped in a characteristically 1920s way, drinking tea in a Chinese restaurant, the red neon sign prominent outside the huge, Hopperesque window next to them. *Sunlight in a Cafeteria* (1958) from the Yale University Art Gallery is another suggesting, brooding interior.

This is a collage of selected phrases from their writing. Anyone familiar with these pictures, or Hopper's work in general, will be struck by how the children have got to the centre of some of his style, of the feel of his works and the emotions he evokes. I think that they have done this more effectively than most adults could have:

> The light looks like a stage light and it looks untrue ... They are looking at the sunset at the end of their house ... it does not look true ... 'Do you think the lights are a little too bright?' ... 'Do you think we are mistaken?' ... They are at the pub. They are at it in the middle of the night. The light is shining in. The lady is looking at her nails. The man is looking at the lady.

Tabitha Tuckett was fourteen when she wrote her '7 a.m. by Edward Hopper'. It is published in *Young Writers 24th Year: Award-Winning Entries from the 1982 W H Smith Young Writers' Competition*: 'Painted sunlight falls on the ticking / Of a clock which shows the window the time, inaudibly. / The window shows an empty street a two-way gaze, equivocal ... '

In another school, Stacey looked at a picture called *Sunday* (in the Phillips Collection, Washington), which shows a lonely man sitting on a kerb on a deserted street. There is the usual Hopper scale and atmosphere: the man is dwarfed by oppressive buildings, and is bathed in an ominous light:

> 'I wish I was in the shop working'. He smokes a cigar. The shop is selling wine. He sits on the edge of the road. The windows are rectangular. The red reminds me of when my nanny died. The blue reminds me of when I was in hospital.

Automat (Des Moines Art Center, Permanent Collection) shows a similarly lonely figure, but female this time:

> She was sad because her husband has left her and it is very bad. The tea tasted like spiders ...
>
> Sarah (7)

Conor studied the most famous Hopper canvas of all, *Nighthawks* (The Art Institute, Chicago), a gloomy study of figures in a bar seen from the street:

> The path is green like lime.
> No one is there
> except them
> people in the pub.
> You can hear
> the water in the plastic
> tubs going g–g–g–g
> The man says
> Can I have a drink of beer?
> I can smell fags in the pub.

The openings of all these writings were done by the children as soon as they had turned over their cards to look at the picture they'd been given, but subsequent lines, such as 'The red reminds me of when my nanny died', 'The tea tasted like spiders ... ' and 'I can smell fags in the pub' all emerged under questioning with individuals later. In all this work, there is much to be gained after the initial stimulus, by pointed and carefully thought-out questions, with long pauses for the child to think further than s/he has already, and to look harder.

Two young women and two young girl writers: Some prose

In another school, a girl looked at a Hopper picture, *Summer* (Wilmington (DE), Delaware Art Museum) and wrote this:

> One day a lady was watching out for a car and a girl because a girl would run in a car and the lady is thinking of her boyfriend kissing her. She has ginger hair with curls. She came out because she was hot. She went indoors because she had a big dinner in a big pot and then she looked outside to see if her boyfriend was there. He was waiting for her at the door and then he went and kissed and cuddled and a bit more kisses and cuddles. And then she said I have eat your dinner because you did not turn up and I could not wait for you and I have had enough of you because you do not turn up and I have to feed the dog too, his name is Pinner. Pinner likes his dinner and Pinner does not want to wait for you OK? Then the boyfriend said OK I cannot help it. I will come round tomorrow and I will be there by 10.30 ...
>
> Katie (10)

I want to link this with another piece written on the same afternoon. Zoe had chosen a postcard of an early Picasso drawing, *Mother and Child and Four Studies of Her Right Hand* (The Fogg Art Museum, Harvard University):

> I think she is holding a baby and she is thinking is he going to grow up a good or a bad baby. She is thinking if the baby is going to tell her off for not having a dad, and if she wants a baby or not. And if she wants a boyfriend or not because she is all confused by having a baby. And she has lots of people around her to congratulate her for having a baby and if she gets rid of it she might upset the people. And she wants a dad because her dad died and her mum so she wants some parents and she loves her parents and she don't want to upset her real parents so she did not get anymore parents so she let the feeling go. And she wants a job but she has to look after a baby but she can get her mum to look after the baby so she got a job. And she looks sad and she looks upset because her mum and dad died but she did not get some more parents she is very upset and sad.
>
> Zoe (10)

We can learn from this writing, if we care to. Both these children are rehearsing, unconsciously, or perhaps semi-consciously, grown-up problems, and thereby preparing for adult life. This is an important function of all creative writing, as it is a function of all creative reading – when they read novels, for example, children rehearse ways of dealing with the predicaments that are presented to the characters. The second of the pieces reveals the intensity of the writer's worries. This intensity is not visible to us in other ways, unless (and it is unlikely amongst readers of this book) we are psychologists or therapists. 'She is thinking if the baby is going to tell her off for not having a dad, and if she wants a baby or not. And if she wants a boyfriend or not because she is all confused by having a baby'. These are extraordinary sentences, and they are redolent of the writer's anticipation of her life.

The confusion of the second piece is its most obvious feature, and it is about confusion. Are the young women's parents dead or not? The horrible phrase 'get rid of it' usually refers to abortion: in the writer's mind, at this point, it sounds as if the baby is not yet born. There is confusion in the first, too: there is a girl at the beginning of the story who simply disappears from it without any comment. Sex in a mild form is there, but then we have recriminations. Confused or not, this child is a more sensitive, a more dangerous observer than her parents have probably guessed. Every child is a spy on his or her parents' marriage, and sees more of that marriage than those of us who are parents would care to think.

Often, I would ask children to redraft their writing. This would have cleared up many of the confusions in these pieces, if not all of them. But by discarding these early drafts, I would have learned far less about the writers and, by extension, all child-writers, than I have. And the rawness of this writing serves an artistic purpose, too. One feels the stories are simply being told, without any frills. The flat style ('And … And … '; 'One day a lady was watching … ') serves to insist on a kind of truth. I feel that the reproductions of the Hopper and the Picasso have opened up feelings that are usually suppressed.

The guilt in the second piece is one of the saddest aspects of this writing: is 'the baby is going to tell her off for not having a dad'? The writer is already anticipating adult events, and the worry and pain that many of them bring. Even the congratulations of 'the lots of people around her' are a source of guilt, because she might 'upset the people'. I note that the word 'upset', linked to guilt, appears four times in this piece of 190 words. Indeed, there is nothing in either piece to suggest the future happiness that the advertising industry, among others, would insist is the prerogative of the young woman contemplating future relations with men and with children.

Danielle was looking at a sixteenth-century icon of Mary and Jesus. The teacher commented in the staffroom afterwards 'That writing is absolutely typical of her'. I think that this piece is a celebration of a girl's relationship with her mother, and that it has been brought about by looking at art. Once again, art is a teacher:

> I love you you're my baby.
> I hope you love me too baby.
> Baby is saying to Mum
> You are my Mum
> you had me in your
> tummy. I love
> you. Mum your
> hands are lovely.
> o baby you
> are so cute
> your hands
> are so lovely.

Another writer studied a photograph of a steam train at an Exeter station:

> At Exeter St David's
> It's dark and mouldy like something out of a nightmare.
> Smoking steam.
> that could choke people.
>
> It's the train of death.
> As it takes off
> it's slow.
> But it goes faster and faster
> until it's so fast
> the people scream.
> The driver laughs.

John (9)

This is, of course, melodramatic. But so what? The reader should worry about over-the-top style, technique and content in a mature writer, but should worry even more about a writer who has never risked these faults. Writing at school should, without doubt, give everyone the opportunity (to put it negatively) to get through this stage. And maybe this stage is what that writer is going to develop into a mature manner.

One boy looked at a reproduction of a Picasso blue period picture of a woman (I forget which one now):

> I saw her standing
> all alone
> nothing there
> but her long cloak.
>
> I saw her standing
> all alone
> nothing there
> but the red rose.
>
> I saw her standing
> all alone
> nothing there
> but the shadow of the boat.
>
> I saw her standing
> all alone
> nothing there
> but the dark blue sea.
>
> I saw her standing
> all alone
> nothing there
> but the sleeping baby.

Everyone finds their meaning in every work of art if they look until it hurts, if they keep listening. It is worth remembering that profound truth of Simone Weil's that I have quoted before: 'Even if our efforts of attention seem for years to be producing no result, one day a light that is in exact proportion to them will flood the soul'. (Panichas (1977:46)). Again, Weil had a related conviction that is worth contemplating in terms of this book: that 'any human being … can penetrate to the kingdom of truth reserved for human genius, if only he longs for truth and perpetually concentrates all his attention upon its attainment'.

9   Art and multicultural education

As I have shown, children write well both *to* and *about* people and objects in photographs and other artworks. Children use writing – poetry, reportage, story, description or whatever – to help themselves to come to terms with an apparently contradictory couplet of concepts that they sense when they are babies: first, how wide the variety of human beings is, and, second, how close to each other, as well, all human beings essentially are. This is true in a general way, and children learn more about this when they look at, for example, Hopper's paintings. More particularly, writing can assist our work in multicultural and anti-racist education; in our understanding of both that closeness and that distance that we perceive in terms of race.

The use of art is valuable here. This is unlikely to be effective as individual paintings are shown to children in a random, casual way. We need to concentrate on one particular artist and his or her setting for a good length of time. This next poem was written by a girl who had been studying a painting by the artist Emmanuel Jegede, who had spent nine days in her school as an artist in residence (see Sedgwick 1989 Chapter 2 for an account of this residency). By the time he left, the children had made an acquaintance with Yoruba culture generally, and one particular Yoruba artist:

> His eyes are the sun
> with a glittery beam.
> His pale-coloured face
> is a sparkling stream.
> His nose is a bridge
> and his face is a dream
> and his cheek is a song
> on his pale-faced stream.

Some schools go to great lengths to educate their children to be citizens of the world. I know from my journeys as a jobbing poet that every Montessori school has, as a matter of principle, a kit about each of the continents. One African folder in a nursery school that I looked in contained, among many other photographs, young Kenyan girls in head-dresses, children in schools in Mali, Yoruba artworks and cities from all over the continent – Kinshasa, Nairobi, Lagos – with cars and buses tearing around huge roundabouts. With the help of international images like these, children everywhere learn at a very early age how they and their neighbourhoods are parts of a varied world. They learn that their topics on 'people who help us' (meaning the milkman, the teacher and the nurse) tell them no more than a local fraction of life's story. There is a world out there with people in it who are both very like themselves, and (equally important) very unlike, too.

Art is an even more powerful way of helping young children to understand the rest of the human race than folders of photographs. Looking intensively at paintings, drawings, carvings, statues, poems, stories, dance and drama, children learn about themselves, the world around them and the relationship between themselves and that world. To help children to establish this habit of looking early, while they are under six or seven years of age, is to do a great duty both to them and to their world, because to pay attention to the world is to know it, to love it, both in its beauties and its ugliness. To pay attention is to learn that, however much the world around us may often baffle us with its difficulties, it is still our world.

I have written before (*Montessori Education* Volume 6 No 1, May 1994) about an African Caribbean artist, Imani (then Paula) Sorhaindo. She was working in a Montessori nursery in Woodbridge in Suffolk. The children looked at and touched artefacts from Dominica: photographs, carvings, clothes, musical instruments. Imani helped them make a collage/painting based on Dominican stories. They crouched on the floor of the nursery, making art together, as human beings have done since the beginning of the race, in caves and rehearsal halls, in theatres and studios.

The kind of work Imani did then is still very necessary in all our schools, because as individuals we are still ignorant of each other. Once, in a largely white part of Norfolk, Imani had sat down to begin a session with some five-year-olds when one of them asked politely, 'What planet do you come from?' Although the teacher was appalled, Imani told me afterwards that she was pleased to hear the question:

> It gave me an opportunity to teach them something very important ... I told them, I come from the same planet as you ... I come from [holding up a map] this beautiful necklace of islands in the Caribbean. I told them, each island is a jewel ...

Part of the task of assuring all children that we come from the same planet can be done by enabling them to draw artefacts from other cultures.

The first communicating act of the human race was to make a mark, not to interpret one. The cave drawing of a horse had to exist before someone else could understand it, or attempt to understand it. But, perversely, we treat children as mark-interpreters – readers, decoders – as a priority. 'Say "c", say "a", say "t"' we demand. 'Read all the words on this card until you find one you can't read ... ' We should not be doing this. We should, instead, be treating children as mark-makers: drawers, scribblers, and writers. Like Maria Montessori, we should understand that children write spontaneously before they learn to read. Part of this writing is implicit deep in their drawings in that they, if we pay them sufficient respect and attention, have much to tell us.

15 A totem-like figure

Six-year-olds looked at a carving from Mali that shows children climbing around a woman. The carving resembles a totem pole. A proud female head looks around at the top. The gentle grain of the wood is visible and the face is burnished smooth. This is in contrast to the hair, which seems to have been made with jabs of something like a chisel or a gimlet, and elsewhere it has been scraped into lines. The children, some of them carrying burdens, wind slowly around the woman, their limbs tangled. Some of the children appear to tread on each other's backs. Before these young people drew the carving, they wrote about it:

> The face is soft, soft as silk. Her hair is bumpy, bumpy as Lego. The children are climbing up her. It looks like they are tangled up so they can't get down from her. It looks like she is thinking, I have these children climbing up me, I wonder what they are doing and why is that child climbing on my hair?

Other five- and six-year-olds had said about this carving:

> If they found a person that's dead, they might have laid it down and made a statue of it. It was a famous person, so they put it in wood and gave it to all the people ... she's thinking the children might die ... if they haven't got anything to drink they might die ... I think the children didn't like the other mummies and they went to this mummy and they climbed all over her because they liked her ... the children are scattering all around her ... she's like a ladder ...
> (from my book *Thinking About Literacy*, Routledge 1999b)

Of course, these hypotheses might be wrong. What matters is that these children are making them at all. As they think and talk, they reflect on huge issues facing the human race. The first obvious one here is parenthood: what is a good mummy? a bad mummy? I'd like to know (or would I?) what went through a child's mind before s/he said, 'the children didn't like the other mummies and they went to this mummy'. The other issues I can identify easily are death and hunger: issues that children confront day by day on television.

Children looked at a story chair from Mali. It is simply two pieces of wood. One is large and decorated with bas-relief carvings of a man, shown twice, trying to catch a fish, also shown twice. The other is a neat little spoon shape that fits through a slot in the larger part to make a comfortable seat. One relatively fluent six-year-old wrote:

> A man is catching a fish so he can eat it and the fish is going deeper into the water and the fish gobbled the man up. The chair is slimy and hard and the seat is shaped like a spoon.

Another wrote

> It good
> its mrvelss
> its sroge
> soft
> dont jrt sad they
> it's sovd like a sake
> it's sime
> its sippree
> its funky

16 A story chair

I have printed this piece as it was written. Immature spelling should not blind us to the quality of thought going on in the writer's mind, and the strength of his aesthetic response. Converted into conventional spelling, it says 'It's good, it's marvellous, it's strong, soft. Don't just stand there (presumably referring to the fisherman and his fate), it's soft like a snake. It's slimy, it's slippery. It's funky'.

The headteacher of the school where I worked with these children said that the fact that the objects were different from those they normally experienced was important. The story chair 'fascinated the children ... They like the unusual ... also, the fact of the size of the chair, that it was large and bold, that held their interest ... ' There is something to learn here. It is a sad truth that most adults like what is the same, not what is different. They are turned on by what is familiar, by what

17 A female head

doesn't shock or surprise them. This means that most of us offer children comfortable images. The jobbing poet sees them almost every day: the Letterland folk, and faded reproductions of Van Gogh's *Sunflowers* or Lowry's Salford. Whatever these images are for, the children largely ignore them. If we were to offer children giant Rothko reproductions, or any other art that most adults reject, we would find that the children, in all probability, would become excited and engaged by it; ahead of us, certainly, in the willingness to work with art in pushing boundaries forward.

Other children have looked carefully at a carving of a female head from Malawi. It is made from ebony. Half the face is the colour we would expect from a rich reddish-brown wood. It's creamy and soft in texture. The other half is black, with thin stripes of the reddish colour. The head is about twenty centimetres high, and heavy rings adorn the woman's delicate ears. The hair is painstakingly done (both her hair, of course, and the carving of it). The plaits rise from the front of the neck, curving round the back of the ears, to join the delicately patterned scalp. The patterns at the back continue and descend to a smooth ebony (though light brown) neck.

Pictures (unfortunately not reproduced here) show us how children can learn from drawing. One child struggles to see how the plaits work, and perhaps her surprise at how she has drawn them is shown in the eyes of the carving. Another concentrates on the plaits and produces intricate detail, to the point where he ignores the rest of the surfaces of the carving. Or – more likely – was the drawing taken away from him before it was finished? He had, after all, to get on with his maths or his science, or some test. What follows is practical demonstration of one of my general principles: **The visual images that children make feed into their words, and vice versa.**

On one occasion, the carving, and a child's drawing of it, released memories of a dream: 'The back of her head is all lumpy … I think about a dream I have', Holly said. We asked her if she would write about it. And Holly wrote on her drawing:

> In my room when I go to bed I have strange dreams. About thin and fat. Feelings lumpy soft. And sometimes they are strange feelings. This model reminds me of those dreams because her plaits feel like those feelings.

A boy wrote about this carving:

> She is bumpy … She is ruf on her nek. She is haf black and haf bwon. She has plat li a bump bisket [plaits like a bumpy biscuit].

Another piece I showed the children is probably the strangest of all the carvings. Two ebony faces are displayed, Janus-like, one looking left and one looking right. One is male, the other female. I have lost whatever words the children wrote about this piece, as well as a marvellously vigorous drawing by a six-year-old boy which took only a few minutes to complete, and which was evidence (I am sorry that you will have to take my word for this) of what can happen when children have courage and we as teachers have allowed them the proper freedom.

Later I acquired two Benin bronzes of a king and a queen. A seven-year-old asked them, alongside a powerful drawing, 'What kind of powers have you? What makes your powers?' and then answered her own questions: 'I make my powers with my head'. Who can put limits to what art can do when placed in front of our children? Who can justify nudging it to the neglected margins of our curriculum, where children, teachers and parents can barely see it? Can't our legislators – politicians, advisers, inspectors – see that art sets children free to reflect on what it is to be a human in a complicated and dangerous world? And if they can see that, do they simply not care? Or could it be that they don't want our children to grow up knowledgeable and sensitive; questioning, sceptical, pushing at the boundaries of the dangerous? It seems likely that politicians and their servants – advisers,

18 Janus heads

19 Child's drawing of Janus heads

20 Benin bronzes

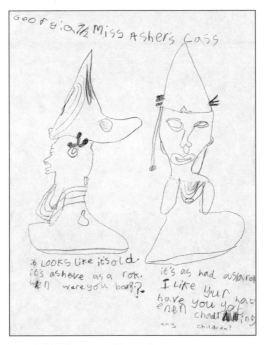

21 Child's drawing of Benin bronzes

inspectors and the rest – want children to be hired hands in a society that has decided beforehand what they should be. A further implication then is that children's teachers are, in the current dispensation, merely hired hands, too.

Looking at art with the intensity that is required to copy it in lines – whether drawing lines or writing lines – is a powerful business. When the art comes from an unfamiliar culture, the learning is even more powerful. The looking shows us that we are all the same – we are merely, and gloriously, human beings. It also shows us that we are all different, diverse, and in great and desperate need of learning about the things we make and call art.

10 Poetry for its own sake

If I were to try to sum up all I have written so far, I would use the words of D H Lawrence, who says that 'the essential quality of poetry is that it makes a new effort of attention and "discovers" a new world within the known world' (quoted in Benton and Fox 1985). I would hold on to that word 'attention' like a shipwrecked *Titanic* passenger holding on to whatever shard of floating wood he or she can find. Education is attention: first, the child's to the teacher. That is conventional wisdom – 'Will you be quiet while I do the register!' – and need not detain us here. Second, education is the teacher's attention to the child. That, of course, is less understood, and bears some serious reflection. Third, there is both the teacher's and the child's attention to the matter in hand. And the most important attention is the writer's, whoever s/he may be, teacher or child, to the language, the medium through which the electrical charges flicker as the learning magically happens. So this chapter is, of course, about poetry that is written with learning in mind, as are all the chapters in this book.

But here the learning is more directly about poetry. Here (to put it in another, friendlier way) the children are merely having fun with words, with rhythm, with all the things that words can do. Here (to be really friendly, to the children, if not to inspectors and politicians) they are *playing*. It is not possible to be a writer at any level without having a sense of the pleasure that words can give, whether they are spoken or heard, written or read. As Freud wrote, 'the creative writer does the same as the child at play' ('Creative Writers and Day-Dreaming', collected in Vernon 1970). Adelman has written about '... the doctrine of original sin with its antipathy to play ... ' and I agree with his implied assertion that philistine perpetrators of a kind of debased puritanism have managed the construction of an ugly thing: our current mechanistic education policies. With all their loyalties to the national economy, rather than to the individuals that make up society, and their relationships with each other, they have built a structure that owes its existence to the love of money, which is, after all, the root of all evil, rather than to the love of our fellow human beings, which is the route to salvation.

All this is not to say that children will not learn about themselves and the world around them when they write in the ways suggested in this chapter. But they will learn that poetry itself is a potent force for understanding about itself:

When I'm riding on my horse
I go fast like a van.
When I'm riding on my horse
My hair goes back.
When I'm riding on my horse
I go clickety-clack.
When I'm riding at the zoo
I feel like I'm rolling down a hill
and I feel like I'm twisling around on the horse.
When I'm dancing
my arms go flip-flap.
When I'm dancing
my arms move like birds' wings.
When I'm dancing
my hair goes like this
[like what?]
like a rocket.
I laugh
When I'm dancing
My dog always runs after me
When I'm dancing

This poem was composed by three children – Jody, who was six, Kelly, who was six and Rebecca, who was five. I asked the children about physical activities, and what they made them feel like. We played poetry games together. For example, I asked them for similes ('What was going fast like?') We used repetition ('When I'm … I'). The children came up with onomatopoeia ('Clickety-clack') and an invented word ('twisling'). The managed to convey the delight in racing along. Older children working on a similar theme wrote the following:

My hairs jump as I first
go into the deep end
splashing like a dolphin
The bubbles crowd my eyes
It stings   splash
As I hold them   my hair crowds
I sink to the deep   my face
dull bottom
No end to where I fall
Jump up for air!
echoes play in my mind xxxxx spin
sink to the bottom
echoes play in my mind
waves to push me to one side

That was a first draft. Here is the second:

> My hair jumps as I first go in the deep end
>> splashing like a dolphin.
> The bubbles crowd my eyes. It stings.
> As I hold them I slowly sink to the deep dark bottom. No end to where I
>> fall.
> I'm lost forever.
> Jump up for air!
>> Echoes play in my mind.

In the same group, a boy wrote:

> Spin fast spin slow
> let the winter wind blow
> spin slow spin fast
> let the spring wind blow
> Spin fast spin slow
> let the summer breeze blow
> Spin slow spin fast
> let the autumn wind blow
> Spin fast spin slow
> let the fast wind blow

Like many of the poems in this book, this was written by a child who was accustomed to failure at writing. The teacher's task here was to inspire him – not with a subject for a poem, but with confidence. He did this by showing the boy that he could legitimately play with the only phrase he came up with at first, adding something new each time. Thus he had the rare and valuable experience of making a little satisfying object on which to reflect.

I often use this poem to help children write in this way:

Kelly Jane Dancing

> When I'm dancing
> When I'm dancing
> My hair flies around
> And I feel the rhythm thumping
> To my feet on the ground.
> I feel my heart speeding
> And my eyes flashing clear –
> My body's alive
> When I'm dancing.
>> (Sedgwick 1994b)

Another way of playing with poetry is to write topsy-turvy poems. By their nature, these poems don't allow clichés, because they insist on using phrases that are the wrong way round, and, therefore, fresh. They are based on 'Tonight at Noon' by Adrian Henri, which you can find in Corbett and Moses (1986:79) and Townsend (1979:185). Or you can simply use this example:

> On a snowy summer's day,
> bananas will eat people,
> a car will drive us,
> the sun will come out at night
> and the moon and stars in the day.
>
> On a snowy summer's day,
> snails will fly
> low in the grass
> and all birds will crawl
> on their hands and knees
> and when the sun comes in
> it will go out.
>
> On a snowy summer's day,
> Antarctica will have a heatwave
> children will cry instead of laughing
> when sad jokes are told.
> People will live on the sea
> and go on visits to the landside.
>
> On a snowy summer's day,
> shopping will buy people
> sunset will be at dawn
> doors without handles will open voluntarily
> and instead of coal fires – ice fires!
>
> On a snowy summer's day,
> kings will amuse jesters
> and tell *good* jokes.
> The sun will shine in a storm
> and snow in the summer's day.
> Jeremy (11)

> Tonight at noon
> children will send their adults to bed
> and mice will chase cats.
> Lions will walk on the streets
> dressed in black and wearing spats.
> Tonight at noon
> snow will fall upwards to the hot sun
> and the first tulip of winter will grow.

In the street
everyone will walk on their hands.

Tonight at noon
Watford will score against Ipswich
10–0
and on the window-sill
potted plants in top hats
will tell each other
about the rocket crash on the edge
of the Milky Way
and the rose bush will run off
to tell the geraniums.

Eloise (10)

Another way of writing perversely, and thereby avoiding clichés altogether, is to write lie poems:

River lies
I have a river in my back garden.
It runs forever round the world.
It is scorching, like an oven.
It carries fire down
to all the places in the world.
Only I can swim in it
for the river is my friend.
After school everyday
I talk to it and it tells lots of lovely secrets.
It knows when floods are going to occur
and when the water level will rise.
In the middle of the night
when my parents are asleep
I go and sleep in it and we talk until morning.
My mother doesn't see us
because the river can turn me invisible.
You can't come in my garden
because the river will burn you
until you run out.
When he goes on holiday
he meets his best friends,
Sea, Lake, Lagoon, and Bay.
I have a river in my back garden.
It runs forever round the world.
It is scorching, like an oven.
It carries fire down to all the places in the world.

Matthew (10)

'I remember, I remember': An exercise in nostalgia

I remember, I remember

I remember, I remember,
The house where I was born,
The little window where the sun
Came peeping in at morn;
He never came a wink too soon,
Nor brought too long a day;
But now, I often wish the night
Had borne my breath away.

I remember, I remember,
The roses, red and white,
The violets, and the lily-cups –
Those flowers made of light!
The lilacs where the robin built,
And where my brother set
The laburnum on his birthday, –
The tree is living yet!

I remember, I remember,
Where I was used to swing,
And thought the air must rush as fresh
To swallows on the wing;
My spirit flew in feathers then,
That is so heavy now,
And summer pools could hardly cool
The fever on my brow.

I remember, I remember,
The fir trees dark and high;
I used to think their slender tops
Were close against the sky.
It was a childish ignorance,
But now 'tis little joy
To know I'm farther off from Heaven
Than when I was a boy.

Thomas Hood

This is a valuable poem for children because:

- it encourages them to recall and therefore learn about significant moments in their lives;
- it teaches them something about the manner of lyric poetry: repetition, listing

elements so that the cumulative effect mounts up; commenting on the elements;

- it teaches them about a common English metre, and offers them some potential experience in it.

How I teach this poem

First, I read it as carefully as I can, milking each line for its effects – lowering the voice darkly, for example, at 'Now I often wish the night / Had borne my breath away' and at 'Now 'tis little joy / To know I'm farther off from Heaven / Than when I was a boy'; making sure that the children know that the line 'Those flowers made of light!' deserves its exclamation mark (or 'screamer' as printers call them); and generally involving myself in these sad reflections as much as I can.

I ask the children questions about the poem:

What memories does the man have about his childhood?

Name the flowers he remembers.

What does he recall about his brother?

What did he think about on the swing?

What childish error did he make about the swing?

Then we play with the poem. The children say it after me, phrase by phrase, copying my style for each line. Then, perhaps, one of them can take the role of leader. I say the poem again, stopping at places and asking them to say the next word.

Next, I ask the children to close their eyes and spend a minute in silence making up sentences for some of their memories. When hands shoot up, I say, can you think of more memories? What about the sense of smell?

I remember, I remember the smell of the hospital ward

The nurses telling us
we were having a visitor
tomorrow.

I remember, I remember
my Mum buying me
a new dress and telling me
to behave when the visitor came.

I remember, I remember
the Princess walking in
and me being in my knickers
and vest as I was chosen
to demonstrate how we played.

I remember, I remember
the Princess bending down
her skirt nearly going
in the paint
but she didn't care.
She then shook the adults' hands.

I remember, I remember
her asking some questions
then saying goodbye.
All that's a memory now
as she died not too long ago.

I remember, I remember
the whole nation crying.
We'd lost our precious rose.

Chantel (12)

Other extracts from 'I remember' poems:

I remember …

skipping to a hundred
on a hot summer day
Dad going, 99, 100 …

Hollie (11)

… my first day at school
my parents disappearing round a corner
leaving me with
unknown faces staring at me.

Alessandra (10)

… smelling my Babbit rabbit …
He smelt of me and only me.

Charlotte (10)

… having blue straps around my waist
and being pulled by my Mum.
The fabric felt all itchy …

Rebecca (10)

… when my Dad dropped me
on the floor.
I went to hospital …

when my hamster used
to climb the stairs.
It was brown and white
and he was called Peanut.

… on Daytona Beach
running across the soft
sand in front of the moving
cars. My Mum shouts
'NO! Stay there'
Then she comes
running across the sand.

Michael (11)

This lesson threw up two memories that we as adults don't believe in. Children often confuse memories with what they have been told, and with photographs in family albums. But whenever I doubt children, I recall that the composer Benjamin Britten claimed to remember hearing the sea moments after his birth:

… being born in a car
a blue Ford
driving to the hospital …

… the first thing I saw
was my mummy's blue
twinkle in her eyes
and she held me
so soft and careful …

… being stuck in a plastic box
after I was born and my
mum holding my hand and
staring into my eyes …

I remember, I remember
Dressing up in a little pink dress
And ending up looking a mess.

I remember, I remember
My first day at school.
I felt all grown up.
I had my Barbie lunch box.
Kiera's Ribena leaked all through.
Everyone enjoyed themselves.

I remember, I remember
My first birthday cake
With pink and green icing.

I ripped off the icing
And gobbled it up.
Unfortunately I felt very sick.

I remember, I remember
My first bonfire night.
I watched the sky sparkle.
I was excited and scared all at once.
                              Selina (9)

I have worked on this idea with reception children, but without reading Thomas
Hood's poem. Instead I have told them about memories of my own childhood.
Then the teacher has written down the children's memories and made them into a
class poem:

I remember when
I had a dinosaur on video.
I remember when
I watched Bad Boys on video.
I remember when
I had a dream of a farm and there was a pig.
I remember when
I was a little boy and I drank from my bottle.
I remember when
I had a dog called Billy and he bit me and Charlie my brother.
I remember when
my cat died and my mum and dad cried.
I dreamed of dolphins and they saved Dennis.
I remember when
I hurt my nose on the wall when Nonny came around.
I remember when
I was in hospital when I was two because I was poorly.

I remember when
I played with the dragon on the computer.
I remember when
I saw a lizard in my back garden licking the leaves on my tree.
I remember when
I went to the doctor's house because I hurt my shoulder.
I remember when
I tried to get a cushion and I hurt my eye on the black table.
I remember
being a baby in my mummy's tummy.

Here are some more simple structures, simple prisons, that set children free on
journeys of discovery:

I went to the sea and I found …

I know an angel/robot/giant who …

Behind the first planet there is/are …

Like many of my techniques, these involve asking children to complete a structure in their own way. There are many other structures like this that I have generated from topics on history and science followed in classrooms, especially KS1 classrooms. The thinking behind this is that the offering of structures sets the emotions free. The relationships between the freedom that poetry requires, and the discipline it also needs, has been put well by Murray (in Lee 1987):

> There is a profound perturbation of the poet's being … the poet gives utterance that is checked from mere exuberance … by the discipline of rhythm and metre.

As well as developing poetry in children, these ideas can be expected to help the teacher to familiarize children with important words. Indeed, keywords in any given classroom at any given time can be incorporated into new structures. It will also help teachers to teach parts of speech: prepositions, for example, in the examples based on 'Behind the first planet … ': 'Inside my head there is … ' 'Throughout my life there has been … '

I went to the sea
and I found
a crab that
was smooth and slimy.

I went to the sea
and I found
a swooping, swirling gull
in the salty sea breeze.

I went to the sea
and I found
a scallop shell
crashing against
the seaweed rocks.

I went to the sea
and I found
a saturated, tattered
message in a bottle.

I went to the sea
and I found
a love for poetry
inside myself.

I went to the sea
and I found
a dirty ragged tramp
hunting for food.

I went to the sea
and I heard
the far away call
of the nesting cormorant.

I went to the sea
and I imagined
the shimmering pearl of wisdom
bobbing up and down
up and down
rested in a silken embroidered
oyster shell
pinky in the evening sun.

I went to the sea
and I heard a small child crying
for his mother.

I went to the sea
and I imagined
the sky dropping
down into the mist
of the wintry waves spraying
over the whispering gallery of the Cobb
                                    Hannah (10)

Another structure is useful for teaching prepositions:

Behind my face
and inside my head
the blood rushes
like people running
to catch a train
in a far-off station
which is beyond the stars.

Through my brain
rattles the days
of the past
and the bad and the good.

Over my mind
passes around the work
that has to be done.

Along the silent path
that is secret
there will be red roses
that are prisoned
in my brain.

Emma (10)

Preposition poem

Before the teacher
   the child froze.
Under the bed
   the rabbits hide.
Beneath the waves
    bright joy is hidden.
Under the sun
    everyone enjoys their world.
Inside the rainbow
   the colours are bright.
Over the clouds
   the gods are rejoicing.
After the fight
   there is no happiness.
Within the hills
   the devil hides.
Beyond the earth
   there are mysterious planets.
Behind the hedge
   the fox hides from the hunters.
To the sun
   is a long spaceship ride.
From the trees
   emerged a spaceship.

Emma (11)

An example from history

Children in one school had been studying the First World War. On the walls were photographs of soldiers and their equipment in trenches. The bookshelves were full of excellent books on the subject. There were also CD-ROMs. The teacher had read the children poems by Wilfred Owen and Siegfried Sassoon. Biased as I am, I suspect these poems had taught the children as much about the realities of the war as all the books, pictures and CD-ROMs put together. Here is a poem that the teacher had studied with the children: Wilfred Owen's 'The Dead-Beat':

> He dropped, – more sullenly than wearily,
> Lay stupid like a cod, heavy like meat,
> And none of us could kick him to his feet;
> Just blinked at my revolver, blearily;
> – Didn't appear to know a war was on,
> Or see the blasted trench at which he stared.
> 'I'll do 'em in,' he whined. 'If this hand's spared,
> I'll murder them, I will.'
>
> A low voice said,
> 'It's Blighty, p'raps, he sees; his pluck's all gone,
> Dreaming of all the valiant, that aren't dead:
> Bold uncles, smiling ministerially;
> Maybe his brave young wife, getting her fun
> In some new home, improved materially.
> It's not those stiffs have crazed him; nor the Hun'.
>
> We sent him down at last, out of the way.
> Unwounded; – stout lad, too, before that strafe.
> Malingering? Stretcher-bearers winked, 'Not half!'
>
> Next day I heard the Doc.'s well-whiskied laugh:
> 'That scum you sent last night soon died. Hooray.'

Then the children had written their poems:

> I am lying in the trench.
> To me it's the waiting room of death.
> After my work is done
> I rest on ice.
> My friend tries to get through to me
> But my senses are lost in my true home.
> I am lost in many thoughts,
> Maybe my last.
>
> I am lying in the trench.
> I ask the memories of dying people to leave my mind.
> I think of my lost children.
> Are they thinking of me?
>
> I am lying in the trench.
> O Lord the Highest
> Will I survive one more day?
> One more day?

My mind is going insane.
Help me anyone, anyway.

I am lying in the trench.
My body is a helpless wreck.
Please help me
Or I'll die.

Steffanie (10)

The books, disks and posters teach what we might call the external history of the First World War. The poetry teaches the children to empathize with the soldiers. In another class that had been studying the First World War, I read three poems by Wilfred Owen. The first was 'The Chances':

I mind as 'ow the night afore that show
Us five got talkin', – we was in the know.
'Over the top to-morrer; boys, we're for it.
First wave we are, first ruddy wave; that's tore it!'
'Ah well,' says Jimmy, – an' 'e's seen some scrappin' –
'There ain't no more nor five things as can 'appen:
Ye get knocked out; else wounded – bad or cushy;
Scuppered; or nowt except yer feelin' mushy.'

One of us got the knock-out, blown to chops.
T'other was 'urt, like, losin' both 'is props.
An' one, to use the word of 'ypocrites,
'Ad the misfotoon to be took be Fritz.
Now me, I wasn't scratched, praise God Almighty,
(Though next time please I'll thank 'im for a blighty).
But poor young Jim, 'e's livin' an' 'e's not;
'E reckoned 'e'd five chances, an' 'e 'ad;
'E's wounded, killed, and prisoner, all the lot,
The bloody lot all rolled in one. Jim's mad.

I do not think there would be any point in asking children to imitate this poem. I include it in my lessons though, and in this book, because it presents as clear a picture as I can imagine of trench life under extreme conditions. I also read them 'Dulce Et Decorum Est' (Owen, *Collected Poems* (1964) p.55). These two poems are useful because they serve to deglorify war. They are also indispensable background to this next poem, which children can imitate.

Futility

Move him into the sun –
Gently its touch awoke him once,
At home, whispering of fields unsown.

Always it woke him, even in France,
Until this morning and this snow.
If anything might rouse him now
The kind old sun will know.

Think how it wakes the seeds, –
Woke, once, the clays of a cold star.
Are limbs, so dear-achieved, are sides,
Full-nerved – still warm – too hard to stir?
Was it for this the clay grew tall?
– Oh what made fatuous sunbeams toil
To break earth's sleep at all?

This poem is powerful because, in contrast to much of Owen's work, it is understated.

I explained some of the terms in these poems. A 'Blighty', for example, is a wound that is not serious, but bad enough to cause the soldier to be sent home to Britain, to Blighty. I define 'fatuous' as silly and pointless. After reading the poems – following much practice at home, and with as much intensity as I can – I asked the children to imagine that they were soldiers in the trench. What would a glimpse of the sun remind them of? Or a touch of rain? Or light? They began to write immediately, and finished these drafts in a short time:

Move him into the sun.
Perhaps he will remember
Going to the beach at Southwold,
Watching the waves splashing down on to the pebble beach
And the multicoloured beach hut roofs,
The sight of endless sandcastles
Spanning as far across the beach as the eye can see,
The photos on the fishermen's reading room wall,
The smell of fresh salt water stinging the wind,
The tiny boats bobbing on the blue horizon,
The lighthouse towering over the St James' Green,
The aroma of Adnams Brewery.

Jerome (10)

This boy used his knowledge of the little Suffolk town of Southwold to great effect, bringing in details that I appreciated more than most, because I know the town well, too.

All the writers found the rhythm and meaning of the first line of Owen's poem stimulating. I think that this is an example of something I do not like to talk or write about, because it seems to me to risk sentimentality: the magic of poetry. Somehow the rhythm of the line combines with its meaning, and the words used by Owen to express that meaning, to seduce the children's minds and hearts, and to help them to write. I can see, in part and darkly, why the line is so affecting: the verb, for example, immediately telling us that the soldier cannot move by himself; and that verb balanced by one of the most powerful of all images, the sun. But still there is much left unexplained in 'magic' and 'somehow'.

Using that magic, the children recalled their own experiences and empathized with that dying soldier and his companions:

> Move him into the sun.
> Perhaps he will remember the days
> when he saw the sunlight
> coming over the horizon.
>
> Move him into the rain.
> Perhaps he will remember
> taking a cooling dip in a river.
>
> Move him into the light.
> Perhaps he will remember
> a candle being lit
> and glowing in the dark.
>
> Move him into the sun.
> Perhaps he'll think of the times
> he ran through grassy meadows
> playing in the sunlight.
>
> Catriona (10)

> Move him into the sun.
> Perhaps he will remember
> waking up on a Sunday morning
> with the sun shining through the window.
>
> Move him into the light.
> Perhaps he will remember
> stepping out of the door
> on a spring morning.
>
> Move him into the rain.
> Perhaps he will remember
> sitting by the fire
> on a rainy day.
>
> Annabel (11)

> Move him into the sun.
> Perhaps he will remember
> the lights on his Christmas tree.

Perhaps he will remember
having a shower before getting dressed
for his birthday party.

Perhaps he will remember
The spotlight at a school play
shining down on him.

Lisa (11)

A musical occasion: Word on the Street

Word on the Street is a pop group. Perhaps by the time this book is published it will be famous. Members of the group told me that they had been on tour the previous week with a group (B*witched) that my eighteen-year-old son knew about (not that he was proud of that fact, being much more interested in a rather harder kind of music, hip-hop). I heard – and saw – the five members of Word on the Street perform in a primary school hall towards the end of 1999. Apparently, agents phone schools asking for opportunities for their clients to perform to young children free in order to build up a 'fan base'. I had been teaching in a room next door to the hall, and had heard the wails and crackles of electronic equipment being tested. I was desperate to resist turning into my father, as all men are: what sort of a racket is that? Will this music have any tunes in it? This is nothing on Lennon and McCartney – now *they* could write a tune. Later, I saw black soundboxes arranged around a rectangle in which the group were to perform. Technicians and managers wandered around plugging leads in, moving loudspeakers and so on.

I stood in the corridor before the performance was due to begin. All the children – juniors – were in the hall waiting, and the group – two young men and three young women – lined up wearing modern gear: the women in tiny T-shirts and trousers, the men in baggy jeans and loose tops. One of the men wore a woolly bobble hat that looked out of place. One of the women wore a large and apparently permanent fixed smile, as if almost demented with good nature. Some of the children were to comment on this later.

Someone – I was still in the corridor, and couldn't see who it was – one of the technicians, I suppose – wound up the children in the hall to cheer and clap, and Word on the Street ran past me and the headteacher on to the little stage. They danced and sang – or mimed, I couldn't be sure – to recorded music. They thrusted at each other suggestively. After their first number, they announced another song. It was important that the boys should yell 'Oh-oh' when they told them, and they told the girls to scream when they told *them*. The children obeyed. The noise was formidable.

The issue about melody – were tunes better when I was a boy, or when my father, or my grandfather, was a boy? – was irrelevant. I had become interested in other issues. The children's attention was complete. I felt that they were both ordered and seduced. They were asked to do things that normally they would have been punished for doing. They seemed to have no problems with this dichotomy, except for one young child who was taken out in tears, and whom I instantly warmed towards. All the others – over two hundred of them – stayed where they were, arranged as if for assembly, transfixed. Most of the teachers seemed to be enjoying the show.

Of course, my grandfather's attention, my father's, mine were as much seduced in their day and mine as these children's were in 1999. 'Bobby-soxers', 'Teddy boys', 'teeny-boppers', 'mods and rockers' or whatever the contemporary slang was, have always been sucked into the industry that is the 'music business'. The only difference, I suspect, was the technology. The power the sound system gave to Word on the Street in that small school hall was formidable; so, too was the contrast (see this from the children's point of view) between the workaday gymnasium and the glamour on the stage, that must have reminded those children of countless television programmes.

The next day, I asked the ten-year-olds of Year 5 to write about the concert. I emphasized the word 'like' to encourage similes and vivid writing generally. The children wrote well, demonstrating yet again the power of first-hand experience:

> The sound was like the blaze of the sun.
> All in, they made you want to scream 'Wow!'
> The dancing made diamonds in the sky.
> A giant was jumping up and down in the hall
> and the men's voices were like the school was falling down. They were like
> comets striking the earth.
> The women's dancing made me feel like the women were me.
> The women's voices were like sweet teddy bears.
> The sound was like we were under attack.
> It made me feel like we were on a boat on a stormy night.
> The microphones were like football cones.
> The girls' smiles were like free animals.
>
> Group poem

Pattern, I began this part of my book saying, is there in all art. I referred to cathedrals and arches, and abstract painting. It was there as well in Word on the Street and their relationship to the children: in the dancing, and the repeated sounds, and the way in which, yet again, the power of the commercial world reduced children to rows of open-mouthed faces, their eyes glistening; yelling and screaming, depending on what they were told to do, and on whether they were a girl or a boy. The pattern is a prison in more than one way.

My own misgivings about the hour-long session go beyond the scope of this book. But writing, I have said, seems to me to be about imprisoning children in techniques and form in order to set them free. In contrast, the children in the hall that day seemed to be imprisoned with no purpose except for what I must call commercial ones: to advance careers (and more than five of them); to sell records. They were also imprisoned in post-adolescent images when they were still children. They were having half an hour of their childhood stolen from them.

Prose interlude
Short stories, and beginning a novel

Children's attempts at narrative are almost always less successful than their attempts at poems. Unless a teacher sees poetry as a joky, pretty thing (see Pam Ayres' books, many of the lyrics of the songs that children are bullied into singing in assembly, and the rhymes in greetings cards); unless a teacher sees poetry as a decoration on the edge of life, rather than an exploration of the centre of it; unless all this, the writing of poems demands freshness. It bans cliché. See, especially, those oxymorons in Chapter 7. It insists on learning, pushing boundaries outwards. **Make it new**, as Ezra Pound told us.

Given opportunities to look hard, to be autonomous, to slip the control of the teachers and other adults around them, children are good at making it new, because surprising comparisons occur to them all the time. They are 'great poet[s] with imperfect tongues[s] lisping perfect verses' as an ancient Chinese poet, Bing Xin, said (quoted in Robert Hull's excellent *Behind the Poem*, 1988, a book crying out to be reprinted). Coleridge wrote that 'To carry on the feelings of childhood into the powers of manhood, to combine the child's sense of wonder and novelty with the appearances which every day for perhaps forty years has rendered familiar … this is the character and privilege of genius … '. Children are poets if they can be grown up, grown-ups are poets if they can be children. The advantage, and there can be no question about it, is with the children. Picasso wished that he could draw like a child.

On the other hand, they have not yet begun as novelists. In their story writing, in which they seem to think (or, more worryingly, are taught) that observation is not necessary, children give way easily to cliché. They use traditional openings without much thought: 'Once there was … '; 'Once upon a time … '. All too often, it should be said, these openings are offered by teachers on cards displayed in the classroom. I collected this list in five minutes in one classroom:

> You might begin your stories in one of these ways:
>
> In a far-off country
>
> It all started when
>
> A long time ago

There was once

This is the story of

The characters are often remixes of well-known princes and princesses, or of children like Hansel and Gretel, and witches like Hansel's and Gretel's witch; and the endings are usually clichés, too: the children arrive home, have their tea and go to bed. Also, children write at length and shapelessly. The skill required to build large structures with language is one of the last to be acquired, and most writers never acquire it. And this length discourages children from the task of redrafting. One might put it like this: from a teacher's point of view, lines and stanzas are easier to teach than paragraphs and chapters.

In story writing, children do not **observe**, or, more likely, they have not been taught to. But the potential for change as you write prose is there just as it is when you write verse. There are at least two ways to get children to break this bad habit in narrative, to look both at their subjects and, even more importantly, at their language. One is to ask the children to write a story in exactly fifty words. This constraint – another example of the prison cell that is necessary in order that art should be set free – leaves no room for clichés or for redundant words. You can point this out: 'then' rarely serves much purpose in tight, narrative prose, and often adjectives are redundant, especially when two are used before a noun, one often too close in meaning to the other to have much point: 'a frightening, scary night' for example. Children frequently write unnecessary sentences in stories, and suggesting they write very short stories teaches them to be ruthless and effective editors of their own and, indeed, each other's work.

I suggest that they approach this fifty-word task without counting words, but with an eye on brevity. They may well come up with stories of sixty or seventy words. The interesting task of pruning then begins. They have to choose which words to keep and which to get rid of, and to choose is always to learn. Ask them to ask themselves the following questions:

- Do I really need this word/sentence?
- Can I say this in a shorter sentence?
- Have I got too many adjectives?

It is worth remembering the following general rules of good prose, which I have derived from 'Politics and the English Language', George Orwell (1961) and altered for children (they don't need to be told, on the whole, not to use a foreign phrase when there is an everyday English one):

- Never use any metaphor, simile etc. that you have heard or read lots of times. This is a large part of the fight against cliché.
- Short words usually make for clearer prose than long ones.
- If you can cut a word – cut it.
- Never use a passive verb where you can use the active. That is, write 'John sailed the boat' rather than 'The boat was sailed by John'.

Here is an example of a superbly tense story by a nine-year-old girl who, it seems to me, is obeying those rules. In it, there is evidence of the girl looking as hard as she might have done when writing a poem. Late in this book, there is still **observation**. Notice the cat's eyes and movement. In my view, there is only one redundant word:

A Death

The house was silent. The dark crept into every corner. Meg's eyes shone brightly in her cat basket. She stretched, uncurled. Meg pawed her pillow and went to sleep again. In the morning she ate and went outside. Meg was deaf and didn't hear the car. The driver wasn't looking.

Abigail (8)

I noticed how this writer had the main event happening outside the boundaries of the narrative: the death of the cat isn't described at all, but implied. And that makes it worse (as an event) and better (as a story). We, as readers, can make that death as terrible as we want. Much as the pictures are better on radio than they are on television, what happens in our minds, implied rather than described by the writer, is clearer and more telling than what is spelt out.

The redundant word, I think, is 'brightly'. What does it add to 'shone'? I emphasize this for two reasons: first because adverbs and adjectives are often unnecessary in writing, not only in writing by children. And second, I think of the educational thought processes that might have gone on in Abigail's head as she searched her story for a word to replace 'brightly'. Another verb, perhaps, in the fourth sentence? An easier option would be an adjective before 'house': 'grand'? 'dirty'? I don't know the answer. But I do know that the thinking would have been valuable.

Here is another example:

The New Pupil

The classroom door opens. All eyes turn. No one dares to giggle or laugh. The new pupil is introduced to the class and to the teacher by the headmaster. Will she cope? Will she get on here?

It will be a test of her maturity. The wheelchair is put in place.

This story was composed by two twelve-year-olds working together (names, unfortunately, lost). Again, the substance, the plot even, of the story hangs ominously outside what we have on the page, leaving the piece to resonate in the mind after we have read it. We are left to speculate about how a child and the other pupils and a school coped. If we are adults, we think about parenthood, and the sadness that we would suffer ourselves, rather than allow any of our children to suffer. If we are children, we think about what we might feel if we were disabled, or if we were a bully, or the observers of a bully.

Finally, a piece of melodrama:

A Murder

A car pulls up outside.
The dark figure enters through the door.
A tiptoeing up the stairs.
All the children are in the front room.
Except one.
A piercing scream makes them shiver.
A rushing down the creaking staircase.
The figure gets into the car.
It speeds away.
Silence.

Caitlin (11)

The other way of encouraging good narrative is to ask the children to begin a novel with a chapter describing the room where the hero lives or works, but without introducing the character. This delays the narrative clichés, all the sentences beginning 'Then he ... ', and makes the children look carefully with their mind's eye. Here is an example:

The Room

I glanced through the window of a neighbouring thatched cottage and saw, if I am not mistaken, the living room. In the corner were bags stacked high to the ceiling. One of the bags fell silently off the top. White powdery stuff was in smaller bags.

The room was nearly empty. In another corner was a light which was the only thing that stopped the whole room from being in total darkness. The gloomy room also had a small oak desk and a grand wooden chair. There was a wide open door at the other end of the room. I could see a couple of paintings through the door on the wall, but it was so dark I could only make out the frames.

I heard a constant drip, drip, drip. Obviously the bathroom was above and there must have been a hole in the ceiling.

A storm began to break out above me. I pulled the hood over my head. I didn't want to leave because I was fascinated that someone could live in this state. Just then two more bags fell. More white powder ... In the room there were no carpets – just plain wooden tiles ...

Jeremy (10)

and another Chapter One:

There I was. I stood in an old house by the entrance to a room. I thought I could hear the house creak. I pushed open the door. A heap of dust fell out. I stood back and let the dust pour out. Once I had stopped coughing I went into the room. The room was so old and dusty my thoughts seemed to echo around it.

As I stood there I noticed a distinctive feature in the corner. It appeared to be the only thing in the room not covered with a three centimetre layer of dust. It was very well cared for compared to the rest of the room.

You may think this strange but it was an old oak clock dated 1795. As I moved near to it, more things became visible through the thick clouds of dust. There were carriage clocks, grandfather clocks, fob-watches and all sorts.

I swept all the dust away from the corner of a large mahogany table. There was a book. I opened it, and on the middle of the first page in big old-fashioned writing it said 'Repair Record: 1783'.

This book was old and fragile, so delicately I turned a page. And there was a person with the same name as me.

Sarah (10)

I like the way both these writers used their first chapter to drop hints about their characters: drugs, I suppose, and an obsession with time. And Sarah's surprise at the end is very neat. Both chapters are examples of a freedom a novelist once described to me: however constrained you are in your life, by financial, emotional and social realities, when you write you are free to make anything happen. You can play with the terrors of the drugs that you have heard so much about, or you can risk going back in time in your own narrative.

This can be followed up by asking the children to write the second chapter. Again, with the aim of delaying the narrative banalities, this might concentrate on their central character's clothes. The third task is to write the last chapter of the book, or the last part of that chapter. Later the truly committed children might build the rest of the bridge between these two structures, though I suspect that will happen only rarely. One child wrote this memorable ending to a novel, of which nothing else had been written (and, to my knowledge, nothing else has been written since):

... I saw that unforgettable, silly purple hat in the crowd around the knick-knack stall where I'd bought the ring. I rushed through the shoppers outside Smith's and Woolworth's and the Cheapskates shop, shouting: 'Neill! Neill!' He didn't look round. I pushed through the little knot. 'Neill!' At last he turned. Someone I had never met in my life before looked at me. A tall girl. 'I'm sorry' I said. 'I thought you were someone I knew.' The girl looked at me for a second or two, and then shrugged. I walked back miserably to the little flat.

Sarah (11)

11 'So help me God'

Poetry and religious education

It is important in our teaching to use stories and images from religion because children should learn about the world and its peoples. The media remind us, year by year, month by month, minute by minute, that we, those peoples, are both similar and different from each other, and religion is the oldest base for both the similarities and the differences. In studying it we examine the tingles that shoot along our nerves when we pray, blaspheme, meditate or wonder. In religion we see the roots of our literature and all our art, and the roots of the literature and art of the whole world. Also, we need to make informed decisions about what is the good life. To attempt those decisions without addressing religion is to live, as someone has said in Gaarder (1995), from hand to mouth. It is to be seduced by a materialism that will surely leave us in the dangerous dark.

I asked a class to write down: 'What does God mean to me?' And I asked children in another class of eight-year-olds: 'What would I ask God if I could ask him anything?'

Why is my Mum always angry when my Dad turns over her show?
Why don't you grant us any wishes?
Why do I wish for things that don't come true?
Why can't I win the lottery?
Why can't I see you?
Will you come to me?

This set of questions were theological in an elementary way, opening the issue that has bothered thinkers of all religions almost since the beginning of time.

Will my brothers ever learn?

This is just one example of sibling resentment that this session threw up.

Why can't I be rich?
How is my future going to be like?
Why can't I do what I want?
Why can't I be the boss of Mum?

Why isn't life the way I want it to be?
When will the school have a real fire instead of pretending there is a fire?
Will school ever end?

I made the same request in a Roman Catholic school, and things became more serious:

My Grandpa wasn't a Christian, can I see him?
What if you never get the chance to become a Christian?

Esther (10)

These two questions were written down by a girl of Far Eastern background who told me that she was worried that her late grandfather, whom she had never met, had died a non-Christian. She also felt strongly, presumably because she has been taught that this was so, that only Christians went to Heaven. The task of framing these questions has given her the opportunity to begin to explore huge, troubling issues. Perhaps this framing has also offered her the beginnings of an opportunity to set herself free from a certain kind of religion that was exclusive and triumphalist. In any case, it seemed to me that it was healthy that Esther had had a chance to explore these issues relatively formally in a classroom. It was certain that she had explored them privately. Connected to all this, another child asked: 'Do all religions go to Heaven?', and another 'What will happen to me when I die?', and I thought of the terrifying sermon in Joyce's *Portrait of the Artist* ('Last of all consider the frightful torment to those damned souls … ') that left all the boys in the school 'in a blue funk', and I realized yet again that these final things still frighten children.

Esther also asked of God: 'If you knew what was going to happen on earth, why did you make it?', which seemed to open discussion of the age-old theological problems of free will and determinism. Such issues are present in young writers' minds, and it is part of the business of teachers to ensure that they are raised. A child who had had a liver transplant in her first year of life asked: 'Will I live longer?' There must have been many silences in that girl's life – in bed just before sleep, in the quiet in the back seat of her parents' car – at Mass, perhaps – when she had asked this question. To ask it in the relative public of a classroom took courage and, in its very openness, will have been an element of learning. Not measurable learning; indeed, learning all the more serious and profound for not being so.

Other questions asked were 'Do people get bored in heaven?', which must have troubled all of us with a passion for jazz and beer in smoky rooms, or the kind of poetry (all of it) that is about how terrible and glorious life is, or the pictures in the National Gallery, all speaking at top volume of how awful life can be, but how unboring. And 'Are the people who crucified you in Heaven?' Are they? How big is forgiveness? How wide are the everlasting arms? This is the last section of this book that I am writing, and I have no time to explore further how children theologize in troubling and beautiful ways. I leave these notes here as a seed that may grow at another time and in another place. As I read what the children wrote, I thought again of a remark of Dylan Thomas's: 'Isn't life a terrible thing, thank God'.

A pot of prayers: a visit to Norwich Cathedral

Children should not be forced to trail around cathedrals, castles, mosques, temples, synagogues and the like holding clipboards that demand answers to questions, or (worse) ticks in boxes. These questions have all too often been dreamt up 'between a sleep and wake' by teachers or, more likely publishers, inspectors and advisers more interested in hitting targets than in children *learning* anything. Children are made to look at a keep, or a stained glass window depicting some historical figure they have heard about in the classroom, and tick a box with a 'done that' air, and move on to the next question, the next little box to be filled.

In contrast, children should use all their available senses – but especially, of course, the sense of sight – to study what they are looking at. If they must carry clipboards, they would be better used for making notes and sketches that they can build on when they get back to school. This grants them a modicum of autonomy, of control over their learning, that is absent when they are filling in boxes with ticks.

The teachers in the school from which this work comes shared my views on this. What follows is a culling of lines by ten- and eleven-year-olds. This session was one of the most difficult and dispiriting I have ever had in my journeys in primary schools. (I once had three consecutive 'c' stream classes in a comprehensive, but that's another story.) The children comprised a group who, unlike their classmates, had not travelled on a residential trip, and who had been offered, and taken, the alternative: two separate days, one in Norwich, visiting the cathedral and the castle, and another on a boat trip on the Norfolk Broads. They had also been promised (I don't like to think of what their expressions must have been as this promise was made) 'a poet' who would help them to write about their visits. My job, then, was to help them follow up these days out by writing about them; by making a kind of sense of them, by putting them in order; by making little verbal objects of those experiences that they might be able to reflect on later.

As I arrived at the school, the class's temporary teacher and their headteacher both worked ominously hard at preparing me for the experience: 'broken homes ... boys in particular have something to prove ... been difficult all through the school ... react to problems with bravado ... '. I sensed my own bravado at this stage. I have taught thousands of classes over the years – this was the kind of thought sequence going through my head – and very few have defeated me so far. I'll start with my poems off-by-heart act – Charles Causley's 'When I was a boy' (Causley 1996:6) – which I've been using as a kind of signature tune for ten years, and then some of my own poems, missing out rhymes, so the children filled them in, thus demonstrating first the power of poetry, and second, their own native wit.

All this worked. I had conquered them, and the headteacher and his colleague had been proved wrong. It was later in the morning that I noticed the bloody-mindedness of almost all the boys. 'Can I see your writing?' I asked one boy. '*Me!?*' (This was shouted, as if my request was a serious intrusion on his privacy. Perhaps, of course it was.) 'Can you be a little quieter?' – 'It was him!' There was a competitive feel about everything that happened, about everything that was a normal part of a classroom. About, for example, who would sit on the chairs that, inexplicably, as far as I was (and am) concerned, were arranged so that the occupants (all boys as it turned out) faced the rear wall. About who would shout the loudest to answer a question. About who could be the most unkind to a nervous reader-out of her poem.

But some story, some old personal myth, concerning dunghills and jewels, resurrection following crucifixion – some such myth came to me then and comes to mind now as I type out this collage, in which everyone has a phrase, at the very least. The point of making this collage was that was no time for the children to copy out, and there were no facilities for photocopying, and I wanted the material for this book.

If I was a permanent member of the staff at this school, I would have made a folder containing words by every writer: *A Collage about Norwich Cathedral*, and published it in an edition of thirty copies. I would have sung the praise of this folder, and of the writers, until everyone in the school had listened. It seems to me now that the competitive awkwardness of these boys, and their negative reaction to me as a writer in their classroom, was nothing to with 'broken homes' or 'bravado' or anything that the headteacher had mentioned. It was more to do with something learnt. Something, depressingly, learnt in the school. Something taught. How often we shy away from that word, as though as teachers we were not responsible for the learning and the lack of it, or, more likely, the learning of the wrong things.

Here are some of the lines the children wrote that day:

> The lines shoot up like beams of streamers crawling up the window ... The lines shoot up like the tunnel of life ... Sounds clash like paint on the wall ... People quietly pray and spirits listen.

> The red candle flickers like it never has before ... like a sparkle of light ... with all the dark secrets of the world ... The wax is like blood dripping down the candle holder ... The cross looms above as if watching us ... wild gasps of amazement fill the air ...

> The chapel reminds me of a dragon's cave full of treasure ... It always has time for your loneliness and unhappiness ... It has room for the prayers of people and is ready to burst out of the building like a bull chained up ... It is small, and you could hear whispers coming from the children ...

> The stained glass windows are like a shattered rainbow. They cast a light picture of harmony upon the cathedral ... [They] look like a flash of the past coming back ... They are like a forest at springtime ...

> The organ is like it's amusing the dead people. It softly plays the music of Heaven ... It sounds like there is a ghost in the building ...

> It's like a pot of prayers coming here. It looks as if it is the door to Heaven ... When you walk on the graves of the dead you hear them whispering deep dark secrets to each other ... The choir sounds like angels floating through Heaven ...

The water and the sun together shine like glitter … Streams flow through ridged edges. They will gently glitter in the water …

One writer made a poem about the cathedral that did not fit into the collage:

> The echoing voice
> travels further than far
> but no further than you.
> The organ plays the soft
> music of peace and paints
> the picture of harmony.
>
> Jessica (10)

In spite of everything, these writers were learning about and appreciating Christian symbolism: the red candle (representing the Reserved Sacrament) hadn't flickered like that before, for these writers … I think there were jewels in the mud, little resurrections after the crucifixions.

In another place, after a visit to a different church, I read to a class of children Craig Raine's poem 'A Martian Sends a Postcard Home' (Raine 1970:1–2) and a child wrote this poem. I have quoted it before (Sedgwick 1997:79), but it is especially relevant in this new context:

> There are men with curses on them
> that hang from the wall on sticks
> with melancholy expressions
> on their poor, cursed faces.
>
> Lotte (10)

'Glory be to God for dappled things'

I read to a class of children Gerard Manley Hopkins' poem 'Pied Beauty', pointing out first that the subject of the poem is, in part, objects – natural and artificial – that have two colours; things that are 'couple-colour', 'brindled' and 'stippled'. I ask the children to listen for words that were about 'two-ness'. I also asked the children to listen hard for alliterative words. I left the children to themselves to discover the real subject of the poem: God's glory in his creation:

> Glory be to God for dappled things –
>   For skies of couple-colour as a brindled cow;
>   For rose-moles all in stipple upon trout that swim;
> Fresh-firecoal chestnut-falls; finches' wings;
>   Landscape plotted and pieced – fold, fallow, and plough;
>   And all trades, their gear and tackle and trim.

All things counter, original, spare, strange;
   Whatever is fickle, freckled (who knows how?)
    With swift, slow; sweet, sour; adazzle, dim;
He fathers-forth whose beauty is past change:
                                Praise him.

I find that the couplings (this technique is especially appropriate, given the first subject of the poem) of double words : 'fickle, freckled … swift, slow; sweet, sour; adazzle, dim' can be usefully emphasized in the reading, and this makes less necessary some of the tiresome explanations. With very little ado, I asked the children to write 'Glory be to God poems', telling them that Dylan Thomas wrote his poems 'for the love of Man and in praise of God' (Thomas 1952) and that the Australian poet Les Murray dedicates his books 'to the glory of God'. The children wrote very freely and with enormous enthusiasm:

Glory be to God
for the steady legs of the beautiful deer.
that carries them through the forest.

Glory be to God
that the cry of the distressed calf
is heard by the mother.

Glory be to God
that the antelope
is so sensitive and alert,
that it saves the herd
from a desperate situation.

Glory be to God
that a cat has the elegance
to leap on its feet
every time it falls.
                    Elizabeth (11)

Glory be to God
for the billions of stars
that light up the night sky.

Glory be to God
for the sunset at night.
and the sun
at the beginning
of the day.

Glory be to God
for cats that fight
when everybody is in bed at night.

Glory be to God
for the horses
that trot along the countryside
and for the birds
that sing on a summer's day.
                    Sammy (10)

In another school, I did this exercise emphasizing the alliteration in Hopkins' poem even more than I had at first.

Praise the Lord
for elephants
trampling, treading
like a wild fire
burning in a tropical forest.
Or a twister or typhoon
not a touch tiny
but tremendously huge!
Praise the Lord
for elephants
stamping, stamping
like storm raining
or like sharks in the sea
                    Chris (10)

I note here how the alliteration makes him look for new, unusual words, and to be playful in his use of them: 'not a touch tiny / but tremendously huge!'

One writer was able to make good use of an obsession, music:

Glory be to God
for music making mounds
or sounds, floating for fields and fields,
woodwind, brass, strings,
clarinets, cellos, trumpets, flutes.

Glory be to God
for louds and softs,
piano and forte,
Beethoven and Bach,
Billie, Blur.

Glory be to God
for classical, jazz and pop,
smooth, slow, soft,
rough, rude, rare,

low, loud and long.
Glory be to God for music.

Hannah (10)

When she had written this, I said to her teacher how I should have read her Psalm 150:

Praise him with the sound of the trumpet:
praise him with the psaltery and harp.

Praise him with the timbrel and dance:
praise him with the stringed instruments and organs.

Praise him upon the loud cymbals:
praise him upon the high sounding cymbals.

Perhaps she was unconsciously influenced by this. One boy exaggerated his use of the word 'e' (incidentally, not alliteration at all, but assonance) and in some ways the effect is ridiculous and over the top. But, as I have written before, in order to learn a new technique in any art or sport or craft we often need to overdo it at first. And I think the poem has an interesting bizarreness. Certainly, if one indispensable condition of a work of art is that it is, as Ezra Pound said it should be, **'new'**, this poem has that condition:

Glory be to God
for the eclipse.
Glory be to God
and very good education
and extreme echoes
in silent rooms
and excellent safety in
England and Europe
and the total darkness
during the eclipse.
Glory be to God
for the total
pitch blackness
during the eclipse
in England. The view was
excellent and extreme.
Glory be to God
for the beautiful extreme
totality of the eclipse
throughout England.
Thank God for the eclipse

and enthusiasm
coming up
to the eclipse.
                    Matthew (10)

Glory be to God
for the rhinos roaming around the African plains
and for big grey elephants
and for sly tigers hiding in the undergrowth
and for lazy lions with manes like shaggy rags
and for tiny rodents scurrying around.

Glory be to God
for giant grizzly bears,
for the mini mice and rats
and slithery snakes.

Glory be to God
for the dolphins gliding on top or under
the ocean surface,
the ginormous gentle giant, the big blue whale,
the angel fish fluttering in the water.

Glory be to God
for the hamsters, gerbils and guinea pigs,
cats and dogs and puppies and kittens
catching balls or playing with string.
For hedgehogs, badgers and foxes
with big bushy tails wafting in the wind.
Glory be to God.
                        Sophie (10)

Writing at Christmas

A bank manager visits Jesus

He enters the stable, briefcase,
waistcoat and jacket,
looking down at the baby,
gold to his eyes.
Joseph is singing 'A penny for a rhyme'.
He looks at Mary crying with joy,
his tears pound coins,
the straw shreds of five pound notes,

Jesus a fortune lying in the manger
made of bronze,
put together
with silver shining needles.
                    Pauline (11)

Here's a way of getting children writing about the central facts of the Christmas
story. I have been developing this over the last ten years from an idea by Jill Pirrie
(1987) who wrote about a class of rural Suffolk children who

> came to the stable as visitors, within a particular role. Within this role, they
> saw the stable through their own needs, preoccupations, interests, prejudices
> even: ... artist, scientist, stable boy, soldier, shepherd ... The imagery of the
> stable would be adapted to the role chosen ...

Pirrie went on to publish some remarkable writing. I show children pictures of the
stable scene – Christmas cards and art books will supply plenty of these – and then I
ask them to be someone different from themselves – an artist, say, or a gypsy, or a
scientist; a sailor, or a soldier, or a teacher. Then I ask them to look at the Christmas event through the eyes of this person. You can achieve remarkable results as
the children struggle mentally to see the familiar scene as they have never seen it
before:

I am an air hostess.
In the stable
the people remind me
of passengers travelling first class.
The star looks like the flashing light
telling us where to go.
Mary's eyes are like scared passengers ...
                    Patricia (10)

The cry of the baby
is music to my ears.
The star, so big,
reminds me of being famous.
The animals' fur coats
are like fancy clothes I've worn.
The new born baby
is full of energy,
Me, a pop star, exhausted,
strands of hay everywhere
scattered, like my fans.
                    Katie (10)

... The crib is like a dugout
where the substitutes sit and rest.
Joseph is like the manager
watching over the team ...

Ciaran (10)

Soldier

The baby's skin
is as soft as milk
and Mary is a beautiful as a rose.
Her lips are red
as the heart
of the Lord's love.

Marko (10)

'Soldier' is obscure as a title here; but note how Marko has brought his Mediterranean Catholicism into his poem with that 'red heart of the Lord's love'.

This next writer saw a dentist visiting the stable. Did she intend the pun on wisdom/wise men? Certainly the water rinse and the surgery light are perfect in their place, and wouldn't have occurred to the writer without this stimulus. She has played cleverly with rhyme:

Here comes the dentist in his sterile white coat.
Straightaway he notices the three kings,
All former patients.
He gets a wisdom tooth out of one of them.
Then he sees the baby as pink as a water rinse.
Soon his teeth will need seeing to
And he will probably scream as most babies do.
He was guided here by a star just as blindingly bright
As his surgery light.
The straw was shredded dental magazines
Thrown out of the waiting room
And indeed the stable was like a waiting room
Crowded with patients, their breathing
Misting the air.
The cattle came to him and are unhygienic, smelly things
That could dirty his suit of white.
He turns them out into the night
To get his surgery ready for this new customer.

Katy (10)

Finally, a resolutely up-to-date poem:

A Computer Technician Visits Jesus' Stable

A floppy disc just waiting for bytes to be transferred to it resembled Jesus.
The sheep, oxen and cows were definitely 3 megabyte ram, he said.
He saw the cradle as a bundle of computer wires.
Outside, CD-ROM that was glistening in the sky was supposed to be a star
    created light for the three robots armed with guns to blast their
    computer game bad guys to smithereens.
The hard drive named 'Innkeeper' stored information on all who visited the
    floppy disc.
The E-mail, addressed to Mary, from the Angel Gabriel,
informed her that she would print out Jesus in 256 colour!

Richard (10) and Nathan (8)

The angels

A church school that I visited wanted me to do some work on the angels' appearance to the shepherds described in Chapter 2 of St Luke's Gospel. They required words written by the children for a Christmas production later in the term. I thought this was in admirable contrast to those Christmas productions that are written by the teacher. I have never understood the point of teachers writing plays for children to perform. It seems to suggest that we are prepared for children to learn about acting, but not about writing. In other words, it misses an enormous opportunity for purposeful writing for an audience. Teachers who, at one level or another are expert at writing (even if it is only notes left for a partner, school reports and applications for new posts) give themselves more practice, while depriving children (who, by and large are not yet experts) of the practice that they need. The thought occurs that the teacher-writer who writes material for the children to perform is high on an inappropriate ego trip; or is, to put it more simply, showing off.

These children had to write the parts that the angels were to speak in their production. I began by reading the relevant verses (Luke 2:8–14) to the children. Then I asked the children to close their eyes and to 'be the shepherds on the hill outside Bethlehem'. I talked about the sheep, the shepherds' clothes, the cold, the grass, the sky. I asked them how, as the shepherds, 'they felt when they saw the angels'. Then, I asked them what they had thought of. I extended each answer as much as I could. For example, when a child said 'I felt nervous' I asked 'Nervous as what? Like what?'

What follows is a selection of sentences that the children subsequently wrote down. Each set of suspension marks indicates a different child's writing. There were, broadly, four kinds of questions: about the children's feelings when they saw the angels, about the noises that they heard, about how the news made them feel, and about what the angels felt like:

When I saw the angels I felt frightened like a new-born chicken … I was as nervous as a sheep meeting a fox … the fear in me was as strong as sudden death …

The noise was like everyone in the world was asleep, there was no noise at all … it was like a silent wind … Then the noise was like the tapping of the rain falling down and touching the ground … then it was like a hurricane …

The news made me feel heartstruck … like a woman having triplets … like my mother coming out of jail … the news made me feel as if I was a statue and the fear was like my heart was stopping …

A wing touched me. It felt like a velvet cloth touching my face … as soft as wool … as a kitten's fur … as a horse's mane finely brushed … or a ring around a planet … I felt like I was in Heaven … The angel looked like a shining miracle … like silvery blanket of snow flying like a bluebird in the cold night air. There was a smell of roses in a field … My ears felt as if God was talking to me …

I have arranged these sentences like this, because that is the sort of activity a teacher needs to do to make the children's words fit into the Christmas production. Then she has the role of an editor, rather than a writer. The children should always be the writers.

As the lesson progressed, the children's writing became stronger and stronger as they shared with each other what they had written, and the lesson came to a climax with the words I have given above: 'The angel looked like a like silvery blanket of snow flying like a bluebird in the cold night air. There was a smell of roses in a field … My ears felt as if God was talking to me.'

Lullabies

I read the children my poem 'Lullaby Jazz for Daniel' (from my collection *Pizza, Curry, Fish and Chips* 1994):

Sleep little baby
   in your wooden cot.
Your mother's gone out
   but your father has not.
He's reading a book
   by the flickering grate
and your mother has promised
   she won't be late.

Sleep little baby.
   God ensures
the planets are turning

beyond the trees.
To outer space
   your worries have flown
and your father reads poems
   all alone.

Sleep little baby
   in your wooden cot.
Your mother's gone out
   but your father has not.
He reads, folded up
   in the big armchair,
then climbs to your room
   to stroke your hair.

Sleep little baby.
   God only knows
what story under
   your temples flows.
Dad's reading a book
   by the flickering grate
and your mother has promised
   she won't be late.

Then I asked the children to write lullabies for children they knew: baby sisters, brothers and cousins and the babies of neighbours:

Sleep little darling
In your neatly cot.
You're so sweet and snug
So sleep as long as you like.

Softly wave the leaves
so gently, so gently.
The air is swirling round you
As though it is your blanket.

The wonderful bright flowers
Are popping out to see you.
But go to sleep now,
You will see them soon.

Children in a Roman Catholic school gave a religious twist to this idea:

Mum's talking softly
Dad's gone out.
Please go to sleep

I've washed you
I've changed you
I've fed you
please rest your head
God has blessed you
he gave you joy
crown him in your heart ...

Sleep tired soldier
you must rest
the war is over
Hitler's dead

Sleep tired soldier
you should be proud
for fighting this war
is so dangerous

Sleep tired soldier
let the angels come
take you home
to Jesus Christ.

Peter (9)

Days

Philip Larkin's poem 'Days' can be found in his *Collected Poems* (1988), but also in the Heaney and Hughes anthology *The Rattle Bag* (1981) that I have used already in this book. The poem is a tiny meditation on time and life, and affects children aged ten and upwards greatly. They too can meditate on these things. Indeed, they already have, long before any lesson in school with you or me. They think deeply in those moments between sleeping and waking; at solemn family times like birthdays of the old, funerals and estrangements. There is an example earlier in this part of my book of very serious meditation, when a girl who had been seriously ill as a baby wonders on paper how long she will live. I have seen children in another school write (when I had asked for 'questions that you'd love to know the answer to, but you don't think you ever will' – see Sedgwick 1999, Chapter 3 for a discussion of this technique) ask 'How does love begin?' and 'How does love break?'

Now Larkin hated children. He suggested a new holiday in the calendar, Herod's Eve, when adults would be licensed to roam the streets beating up any young people they happened upon, and he remembered as a revelation the discovery that it was not people he hated, but children (Larkin 1983:114). Nevertheless, much as he would dislike the notion, or be surprised by it, he offers children here an opportunity to meditate in the little prison of a lyric; to observe, for a moment, not the phenomena of the natural world, or the artificial one, but on less tangible realities:

Days are for the loving of
The hating of
The worrying of
Days are for peace and war
Light and dark
Day and night
There for old, young, big, and small.
So enjoy days before they end.

Linnet (10)

In studying religion, I have written above, children examine the tingles that shoot along their nerves when they pray, blaspheme, meditate or wonder. In religion, I have suggested, they see, or at least sense, the roots of all their literature and all their art, and the roots of all the literature and all the art of the whole world. I hope that this part of my book shows how children reflect readily on God and the big issues that crowd on them – if we as teachers accept our responsibility to let the children be fully human. We have to teach in the spirit of something David Gascoyne wrote: 'Truly to be Man is to be Man aware of Thee / And unafraid to be / So help me God'.

Appendices

1 Bringing living poets into the classroom

'Fine art is the only teacher, except torture'

George Bernard Shaw

'Here comes the poetry man!'

Child in an infant school

Throughout this book, I have suggested ways in which poets – Shakespeare, Christopher Smart, William Blake, Thomas Hood, Wilfred Owen and others – can come into your classrooms and teach your children. They will do this for the price of one of many anthologies (see References). It would be even better to get their *Collected Poems*, or a good *Selected*. Combine one of these poets with some passion, commitment and humility from you, and poetry is a teacher, and great poetry is a great teacher.

A strange fact should alert us to the power of poetry: it does not die. Poetry readers talk conventionally about good poets, whether they are alive or dead, in the present tense, not in the past. They say 'Shakespeare says' rather than 'Shakespeare said' and 'Christina Rossetti writes' rather than 'Rossetti wrote'. This is because Shakespeare and Rossetti live on in their loves, passions and obsessions when we read their poems, and thereby make those poems ours. Nature and all its produce rots and dies (not least, of course, the human body) and children are fascinated by that process; but poets and poetry lives on. To put it in Shakespeare's words, although 'Devouring time ... [blunts] the lion's paws', poets, in contrast, live eternal in their verse 'ever young'. 'So long as men can breathe or eyes can see, / So long lives this [the poem] ... ' (Shakespeare, Sonnets 19 and 18). It is not possible to overstate the power of work done in terms of that potent triangle: the receptive child-writer primed to respond and make a poem his or hers, the passionate teacher, and the great living/dead poet.

But it is also possible to bring poets into classrooms who are alive in the literal sense. They may well not be great: no one will be able to say for a century or two, however much critics and journalists, with their league tables, pretend otherwise. A great poet is merely one that most people agree is great. But writers are working at the moment, with anything from a nervous uncertainty about their work to a scary confidence. They bring the scent of the active poet into the classroom. Practically, they are an enrichment to any school because they know ways of starting poems. This is partly because of their own experience as writers. They have, after all, sat often, with a silent desperation, in front of blank screens and blank sheets of paper, wondering if there will ever be another poem, or another story. They know about writing. They have written anything, but *anything* – notes about football matches, educational books, articles about education and social policy, reviews, essays of all kinds. They have hacked their way down the dimmest alleys off Grub Street to pay the bills and to keep their hands in when the poems wouldn't come.

The first time I saw the power of the living poet in the classroom was when a member of my staff, back in 1982, invited Kevin Crossley-Holland to talk to his children. The children became almost as obsessed with Anglo-Saxon words and things during the short residency as Crossley-Holland himself was, and my guess is that some of them, at least, will never forget those days. At one point, Crossley-Holland ran his dampened finger tip round the rim of a Saxon goblet, and made it sing. I wish I still had the poems the children wrote that day.

Most writers are also decent types with a sense of humour, who add something to the staffroom as well as the classrooms. Their visits demythologize the art of poetry. This is first because they look like the person next door, only less well-dressed and more nervous at the beginning of the day when they arrive, and more relaxed at the end, when they drive off in their tired little Nissans. Second, they look like teachers. Indeed, a large number *were* teachers, and even headteachers – until they were found out. Some writers have an impressive fund of dubious limericks in their heads, and will tell you a few for an extra consideration, often for as little as a pint of the local bitter, or a gin and tonic. They will run workshops for teachers, parents and governors after school, and the poems written will vary from the thoughtful and almost sublime to the scabrous and hilarious.

Your local Arts Council Literature Department will find you names and numbers of writers, and so will the Poetry Society (22 Betterton Street, London WC2H 9BU).

What follows are some suggestions for dealing with the visiting writer.

Support the writer. This may seem obvious. But I write these notes in the first-hand knowledge that sometimes a writer struggles like a salmon against the stream, without the salmon's God-given and justified confidence. This is a nasty feeling, only softened by the knowledge that the writer (unlike the salmon) will be out of here soon. So don't give the writer cause to think like this.

The writer probably wants to know on arrival (especially if s/he has travelled more than sixty miles) where the loo, toilet, lavatory, comfort station, rest room, or whatever you call it in your school, is. S/he would also like to be offered a cup of tea or coffee. If the distance the writer has travelled is more than a hundred miles, a cheese roll from the local bakery would probably be very welcome. These are all, in a sense, trivia, of course. Man cannot live, famously, by bread alone. But they are, in another sense, basics. The writer may feel rough in front of a class if s/he got up at six in the morning and hasn't breakfasted.

The most difficult situation a writer faces builds up something like this: someone (the writer knows who it is, probably the headteacher, or the language co-ordinator/ manager, or whatever they're called by the time this book comes out and is read, or someone who attended with creditable and, at the time, encouraging enthusiasm, one of the writer's courses) has decided that some of the teachers in this school (it is soon obvious who *they* are) don't do enough 'creative writing', or poetry; that they are too locked into the secretarial details of the literacy strategy. That they think that writing is really punctuation and spelling.

In a classroom run by a teacher like this, the writer is in the missionary position, and spitting (or worse) into the wind. If you are the teacher who has invited the missionary-writer/poet, keep encouraging him/her in his/her work. Insofar as time and the school's organization allow, see what the children are doing in his/her lessons. At coffee and lunchtime, ask about and, if it is in your power, show genuine enthusiasm for it. If you are one of the baffled savages ('What do we want a poet for?') – unlikely, I admit, if you've got this far in my book – suspend disbelief and accept for the day that a child who writes a vivid poem is also likely to progress in other aspects of English. One seven-year-old asked me today, as he finished the tenth line in a list poem ('Things I saw on the playground today') why did I think that he had finished a whole page, while normally he wrote only two or three lines? The answers to this (there are more than one of them) are worth the savage's pondering.

If you are a baffled savage, here is a plea: do not sit at the back of the class, put your feet up on a chair and ostentatiously read a book about an important subject, such as Technology in the New Millennium.

The missionary position, I am glad to say, is unusual in most schools. The rest of this part is about poets in schools in more congenial settings.

Stay with the writer while s/he works with your class. This is the correct strategy for three reasons: first, the writer, whatever s/he might know about writing, humankind and its problematic relationship to the glory of God, knows nothing about your class. S/he does not know, for example, who has asthma or epilepsy, or which savage beast is calmed by gentle words, which with firmness, which with music, which with bribery. S/he does not know who has just come back from an exclusion, or whose parents have just been divorced, or whose grandmother has just died. S/he does not understand the tears and laughter as you do. And in any case, the writer is not responsible for discipline.

Second, note that the writer is hoping to learn something from you: your classroom management skills, the way you use humour, the way you defuse awkward situations between children. In return, you might learn something from the writer. What might you learn? About teaching poetry, first. Nipping out to make phone calls speaks volumes about your commitment, or lack of it. It is deeply depressing, as a writer working with children, to see the class teacher slip away, closing the door behind him or her, grabbing a rare chance of a free period. If you stay, you might learn, too, about the nature of the rapport between a teacher with a passion and a class s/he doesn't know. This one-day stand can be a surprising liaison, and more full of love and passion than many another one-night stand. You might also learn that in spite of your prejudices against yourself, or against poetry, you can write.

And, in any case, third, should you leave your class with a stranger? This is a professional matter. So is the following, one I have already hinted at: do not get on with minor (or even major) administrative tasks while the writer is working with your class. If you are tempted to do this, reflect for a moment on what you are teaching your children while you sit at the back of the lesson filling in special needs assessment forms, or job applications or pools coupons or betting slips or whatever. You are teaching the children, intentionally or not, that there are more important things than this writer's work, and (look, children) I am doing them (tick, tick, tick, cross, cross, cross).

Also, and I know this is special pleading, it is very discouraging for the writer when s/he discovers that, during the lesson, you've been in the office on the phone organizing your school's ties in the forthcoming town football or netball cup competition, or arranging INSET on the latest government fad. No. Far from clearing off and tidying the stock cupboard, a really involved teacher gets stuck in. Gets stuck in to extent of writing alongside the children, and looking at what the children are writing, and making suggestions to them. This is teaching. It teaches those children that writing is a valuable activity, and not merely something that only children do because adults tell them to.

A writer will feel pleased if you look at the books s/he has probably left neatly in a little display in the staffroom. Do not pick one up, flip through it and say 'Looks a bit "meaning of life" to me'. It is best, as well, not to count the poems in the slim volumes of verse, look at the price and murmur to your neighbour 'That's 27p per poem!' in a stage whisper. Above all, do not approach the writer with fifteen pages of a book in between the finger and thumb of your hand and say 'I'm afraid we're rather hard up at St Margaret's – could we photocopy this bit – it suits our topic for next term'. If provoked too often in the way, many a writer will respond gruffly with 'Sure – as long as I can pick flowers from your garden, raid your fridge for my dinner, steal your liquor … '. All these 'do not' stories are based real experiences of mine.

If you want your writer to feel at home, conversation and buying the books are the best way to do it. If your writer is staying in the area for one or more night, give him/her space. A room in a reasonable hotel or bed and breakfast establishment is appreciated. You should pay for this. If s/he has booked into some anonymous B&B, or TravelLodge, do not say 'Surely you'd like something more personal, like our one of our governors' homes'. Believe me, shocking as the fact may be, it's almost certain that s/he won't. S/he is enjoying the anonymity. 'No, something *less* personal, *less* personal', as one writer exclaimed when faced with this supposition.

If the writer stays at your house, do not expect him or her to be on call all the time to meet teachers from other schools to answer questions about whether this sort of thing works with special needs kids, or whether there is space in the new curriculum for things like poetry and art, or whether s/he would like to see some poems your aunt wrote before she died aged 97 in Worthing last year. Here are the answers: It does, there'd better be, and no, a thousand times no. The writer should not be quizzed in this way when he has a poem or novel or article to write or read, or thoughts to think, or prayers to pray, or a football match to watch on the television, or a pub down the road s/he's noticed that doesn't look too bad and that serves the local bitter which he or she has never drunk.

By all means, use the school's computers to publish for children, staff and parents an anthology of the poems the children write while inspired by the writer. This is a valuable educational thing to do because it shows the children how much you value their work, and it also teaches them something about publication. It is best to print as many copies of this collection as you can afford, in order to approximate as closely as possible to what the children will think of as real-life publication. But – and this is important, admittedly to a tiny minority of writers – if his name is 'Fred', do not call that anthology 'Write Said Fred'.

Let me quote Sandy Brownjohn on a sensitive subject:

> the writer should be paid on the day he visits … making him wait, sometimes for months, seems to be merely bad manners. Even if the money if coming from your LEA it should be possible to arrange payment on the day.

Yes, and your writer should probably not be taxed. Most writers do not pay tax as they earn; they pay lump sums at the end of every July and January. If they are taxed by your school, or your authority, they have to recover that money at the end of their financial year. This seems to most of them to be unnecessary clerical fiddling.

2   A word about learning by heart

This note, adapted from an article I wrote in Wilson (1988) and also corrected, is included especially for teachers who are passionate about poetry themselves; who are brothers and sisters in the mystery; who have learned poetry by heart. It has become clearer and clearer to me over the years how unusual a passion for poetry is, how strange it seems to most people, teachers included. I mentioned a book of poems that I had written to an education officer, and he held his hands up, palms outwards, in desperate defence, practically calling for garlic. He probably felt, along with Nigel Molesworth, that 'Poetry is sissy stuff that rhymes' (Willans and Searle 1958) or that it had a kind of dubious magic. Most people are negative about poetry. 'Poetry's unnat'ral; no man ever talked poetry 'cept a beadle on Boxing Day' (*Pickwick Papers*).

There may only be a few enthusiasts, a few brothers and sisters, but those few count. They are a delight to meet. Some of them know anthology pieces from their childhood, such as 'I remember, I remember'. Others ask where they can find a poem that they haven't seen for years. Others actually pick up the poet's books and read bits out to each other. Others talk knowledgeably about a poet they admire, and whom they have been reading for most of a lifetime. This section is especially for them, but it is also included for those teachers who are interested in the argument about learning by heart/rote. It is for teachers (all teachers, I believe) who have someone in their class, maybe as yet unidentified, who learns poetry by heart at home; who is, one day, going to be a poetry obsessive.

I am going to begin this reprinting by quoting the poet Michael Donaghy, who was talking on the *South Bank Show*: 'No one ever gets a novel by heart. "By heart" means something, because to write for the heart, to learn by heart, is also to write from the heart and that has to go deeper than writing for and from the head'.

The first lines of poetry I learned off by heart, apart from hymns, were:

> The curfew tolls the knell of parting day,
> The lowing herd winds slowly o'er the lea,
> The ploughman homeward plods his weary way,
> And leaves the world to darkness and to me.

Mr Ball wrote the lines on the blackboard in his immaculate cursive hand some time in 1955, my last year at primary school, and he told us to copy them out as neatly as we could. I was delighted. I knew the lines by heart already, because my mother used to say them to me in her Irish voice, over-emphasizing mechanically every other syllable: 'The *curfew tolls* the *knell* of *parting day* ... '

Not everyone had such a happy experience. Brownjohn recalls (1982:86)

> the last minute panic of memorizing often unmemorable lines; the interminable mumbling and stumbling as one by one you stood to recite the *same* poem; the artificial choral speaking with flourishing of arms and voices ...

'How odd' Brownjohn continues 'that usually the worst poems stay in my memory ... '

By the time I was fifteen, some of the poems I knew were awful, like a piece of Longfellow. I found 'The Dying Slave' enormously affecting. 'Beside the ungathered rice he lay / His sickle in his hand / His breast was bare / His matted hair / lay buried in the sand': that romantic failure, that heroic defeat was the best I wished for at the time. If I could manage that pose, that was the most I could do. Rather better was: 'Creep into thy narrow bed / Creep and let no more be said'. Matthew Arnold wrote that, in another of my mental anthology poems. I tried once to make my mother say her favourite poems less mechanically. But she'd been taught to say them her way, back in the 1920s, and that was right then, in Co. Cavan, in Ireland.

I also knew hymns by heart, partly thanks to my mother again, and partly thanks to New Park Road Baptist Church, where I had been sent for my doses of Billy Graham and guilt. 'There is a fountain filled with blood / Drawn from Immanuel's veins / And sinners plunged beneath that flood / Lose all their guilty stains.'

Later, I realized that I had a magnetic memory. I have a litter bin in my head full of lyrics of Adam Faith and Cliff Richard singles. I'd gladly empty it into a skip if I could: I can't hear the word 'easy-going' without slipping into Adam's hit of around 1962 with that word in the title. Would you like to hear how 'The Day I Met Marie' goes? Nor would I.

But my brain also contains much of Philip Larkin's two middle books: for example, 'Talking in Bed', 'No Road', 'Maiden Name' and 'Dockery and Son'; and loads of early Yeats. Like Larkin himself, I only came across the later Yeats in adulthood, just before I lost my by-heart powers. What a glorious shock these lines were when I came across them in my thirties, just before that happened:

> Never to have lived is best, ancient writers say;
> Never to have drawn the breath of life, never to have
>   looked into the eye of day;
> The second best's a gay goodnight and quickly turn away.

By my late teens, there was plenty of Hardy in my head, and, in the most honoured places, George Herbert's 'Love bade me welcome but my soul drew back' and Shakespeare's 'My mistress' eyes are nothing like the sun', probably my two favourite poems. By now my mother's influence, at least as a poetry enthusiast, had waned, and I was reading what I had to study for 'A' level (Yeats and Hopkins) and what a boss in my first job recommended (Larkin).

I acquired most of these poems in a few minutes each without really trying. And I have spent many happy solitary hours walking country lanes, beaches and city streets thinking of whole poems and saying them to myself. I tend to mouth the words, and have got some odd looks from ploughmen, surfers and boozers home-ward plodding, but it seems an innocent occupation compared to being a mugger mugging old people, or a politician or an inspector terrorizing schools.

But recently, and here this piece turns a serious corner, I tried to commit a Hardy poem to memory: one I'd not come across before. I was at my in-laws' house in the Potteries, and the family was out at the municipal swimming baths. I can't swim, so I thought I'd better try to do something useful. I got the twelve lines of Hardy into my head in about two hours, and two hours later, they'd slipped away while I was thinking of something else. The family came in for lunch, and, to compare to their glistening health, I had nothing to show for all my effort. Now I can't even remem-ber the first line of the poem, to look it up in the *Collected Poems*. I can't do it any more! My memory has lost its magnet. Talk about intimations of mortality.

It saddens me to know I'll never get, by heart, any of Shakespeare's sonnets except the three I've known by heart for half a life: 'My mistress' eyes', 'Th'expense of spirit' and, of course 'Shall I compare thee ... '. While I had that magnetic memory, I should have taken more in. I have no Edward Thomas: I can't get 'Old Man' or 'For you Helen' by heart, however hard I try. I came to love his poems after my by-heart powers had failed.

If I were asked to advise young people about learning poems, the first thing I'd say is, Do it. Now. While you are young – you'll need these poems later. '... poetry' (Brownjohn again) 'used to be spoken and [used to] enthral so why should it not do so again? Children learn songs easily, but there is also music in poetry ... '

This belief in learning poems is a bit odd for me. I am a teacher of the Plowden generation, stereotyped a 'progressive' by the *Daily Mail*. (How do you define art? It's something the *Mail* disapproves of.) I abhor streaming and see children as 'ac-tive learners' rather than passive receivers of adult wisdom. So rote learning ... ? No. That's wrong. It is by-heart learning, which is something different. It means learning with joy and emotional involvement, and it doesn't involve detention if you don't do it right in class the next day.

Sandy Brownjohn puts her finger on something important when she emphasizes that children should choose the poems they learn off by heart:

> About two thirds of the class participated and their choices were extremely varied and interesting ... Some poems were complex and adult, perhaps not fully understood by the children ... chosen for their music ... and an intuitive sense of meaning and quality.

This should remind us, once again, that choice is always educational. Why not let children choose the poems they learn? As they think about the qualities and appro-priateness of one poem over another, they are thinking seriously about each poem and things like rhyme and meaning. They are thinking, too, about the relationship each poem has with themselves. And why not go further, and play games with poems in class? Any of the pieces given in this book would work: I have chosen them not only for their stimulating qualities for writing, but for their memorableness.

Second, I say it's best to concentrate on short lyrics. I would be very worried by someone who could do pages of Pope, Dryden, Milton or even Wordsworth, and didn't have a Donne love poem, or 'The More Loving One' by Auden. This latter is a perfect poem for saying on country lanes on clear nights in summer, much as Yeats' 'The Wild Swans at Coole' should be kept for autumn days near water. As far as Shakespeare is concerned, learning poems for young people should mean less 'Once more unto the breach … ' and more of the songs and lyrics: 'Fear no more', 'Ye spotted snakes' and

> Full fathom five thy father lies;
> Of his bones are coral made:
> Those are pearls that were his eyes:
> Nothing of him that doth fade,
> But doth suffer a sea-change
> Into something rich and strange.
> Sea-nymphs hourly ring his knell:
> Hark! now I hear them, – ding-dong, bell.

I have taught infants Puck's lines from *A Midsummer Night's Dream* (Act 3, Scene 1) that begin

> I'll follow you: I'll lead you about a round,
> Through bog, through bush, through brake, through briar;
> Sometime a horse I'll be, some time a hound …

and got the children learning the little jerky phrases by heart. They'd also learned sections of 'Ye spotted snakes' and written lullabies for themselves:

> Oh wasps
> you black and yellow wasps
> dont sting me
> oh spider
> dont spin a web round me
> oh whale
> dont lay on me
> dont crush me
> oh ghosts you white ghosts
> dont take me to your castle
>   Carl (6)

Writing like this is another way of taking on Shakespeare 'by heart'.

So I cannot memorize poems anymore. 'Not for this / Faint I, nor mourn, nor murmur: other gifts / Have followed; for such loss, I would believe, / Abundant recompense' (Wordsworth, 'Tintern Abbey') Though I can no longer get poems by heart, I can, of course, do other things with them that I couldn't do then. My understanding is more potent, and I hear, see and taste what a poet is doing in a way I didn't as a young reader. A teacher at grammar school told us that Gray's 'Elegy' sentimentalized the 'rude Forefathers of the hamlet', and I understood what he meant. The 'rude Forefathers' and their 'homely joys' seemed a fraction patronizing, and the tone wasn't improved by the conceded possibility that 'Perhaps in this neglected spot is laid / Some heart once pregnant with celestial fire'. Other ways of looking at (and, indeed, learning) poetry were awakened. I became analytical, critical, sceptical. But quite often I'd rather have love for the words, their sounds and their rhythms, for any amount of Leavisite correctness, or post-modern alertness.

I visit Stoke Poges every summer because of my journeys as a jobbing poet, and read the stanzas from Gray's 'Elegy' on the poet's huge rather showy memorial. Among the hundreds of graves, there are few more poignant than those of local children who died in an accident in Cornwall while on a school trip a few years ago. Young people need to know that they'll need poetry later on, when they face up to such things. Every year I read those words aloud:

> One day I missed him on the customed hill,
> Along the heath and near his favourite tree ...

and think of the drowned boys buried a hundred yards away in the same churchyard, and hope that among their consolations, the families find the words of a poem here or there.

3 A selective glossary of terms useful in teaching writing

All definitions are from *The Longmans Concise English Dictionary* (1985)

Alliteration

'The repetition of usually initial consonant sounds in neighbouring words or syllables'. This is useful for teaching children something about the inherent music of poetry. Used to excess in the early stages of a school year, it is enjoyable, educational and important but, as with beer, garlic and irony, moderation becomes important very quickly. Examples: 'The waves hiss and sizzle on the sea shore'; 'A bald bat's beak from Budapest'.

Assonance

Best defined as the same as alliteration, but with vowels rather than consonants. In its similar contribution to the music poetry makes, it is a useful alternative to rhyme (see p.195). Example: 'Joan moans her holy groans again.'

Cinquain

See 'syllables'.

Cliché

'A hackneyed phrase or expression'. Awareness of clichés, and the resultant avoidance of them, would, I believe, contribute more than anything to improving the quality of children's writing. You don't want them writing (or even saying) 'the cat's fur was nice, like silk'. To make children aware of what clichés are, and, by extension, how important avoiding them is, play a cliché game. Re-reading this at a later stage, it occurs to me that it might be best to do this activity on an INSET course with teachers first, and then offer the children the results from that. Then talk about phrases the children have heard many times, such as 'sick as a parrot' and 'over the moon' (football is always good – too easy, really – for a crop of clichés). Ask the children, in groups of five or six, to amass a collection of these phrases, then see which group has collected the most. Put them on the wall with a massive X through them. Here is a list of clichés to get them going:

like a scalded cat

news spreading like wildfire

sworn enemy

plain as a pikestaff

at the end of the day (meaning when all has been sorted out)

in this day and age

level playing field

As I write, someone says on Radio 3 that the part of Don Giovanni *suited* [this singer] 'like a glove'. This pushes the cliché issue further. The traditional cliché is, of course '*fitted* him like a glove'. This example is of a cliché so deeply bedded down in the speaker's mind that she slides over it without even reflecting on whether she's got it right.

I address the issue of clichés at some length in my 1997 book (pp. 59–61)

Draft

This valuable word should become part of the everyday discourse of the classroom, in requests like 'We are going to make our first drafts now' as opposed to 'We are going to write a poem now'. 'Things are never definitively in order' wrote Alain Robbe-Grillet, and the notion of drafting reinforces this important idea. Children should be encouraged to write as freely as they can, not worrying about spelling, punctuation and grammar, and certainly not using rubbers to erase supposed mistakes.

Children's second drafts should happen on top of their first draft, with correction marks, arrows, lines, asterisks. It is not fair and it is not educational either to ask children to draft and redraft until the thing is eventually perfect: a daft notion anyway. What on earth is a perfect poem, or a perfect story? Copying out is of no educational value.

I deal with the issue of drafting at greater length in my 1997 book (pp. 61–7)

Haiku

See 'syllables'.

Metaphor and simile

Metaphor is 'a figure of speech in which a word or a phrase literally denoting one kind of object or idea is applied to another to suggest a likeness or analogy between them'.

Simile is 'a figure of speech that compares two unlike things; usually uses the work "like"'.

When you write 'The cat's teeth are like—', you are writing a simile. When you write 'The eyes are—', you are writing a metaphor. You are saying something *is* something else: 'The cat's eye is a big green marble', for example.

Parts of speech

NOUN

Comes from the Latin *nomen*, name. Thus a word 'that is the name of a person, place, thing, substance … ' Used to be called 'a thing word'.

VERB

A word that expresses 'an act, occurrence or mode of being'. In popular infant parlance, of course, it is a 'doing word'.

ADJECTIVE

'Word that modifies an noun or pronoun'. A 'describing word', of course.

PREPOSITION

A word or phrase 'that combines with a noun, pronoun etc. to form a phrase with relation to some other word'.

ADVERB

'A word that modifies another word' – usually, but not always, a verb.

Note that all sentences need at least one noun, or a pronoun ('I', 'she', 'they' etc.) and at least one verb. Adjectives and adverbs are not necessary, and are frequently unrequired baggage, as in 'the *naughty* scoundrel' or 'the *frightening* nightmare' or 'smiling all over his face, he ran *happily* … ' Children should be taught to be wary of these parts of speech. Getting into the habit of questioning the value of every adjective and every adverb will make their work tighter and more muscular.

Here is a cautionary tale, told to me by my friend Andrea Durrant, who was working at the time as an adviser. She watched a teacher of ten-year-olds talking to her class about adverbs: 'An adverb is a word that usually ends in "-ly". It *qualifies* a verb … it says more about the verb in its sentence. For example … '

Here she wrote on the board:

I run to the beach quick*ly*.

and

I walk to the bank slow*ly*.

'"Quick*ly*"' the teacher continued 'and "slow*ly*" ... Both tell us how I *ran* or *walked*. Can anyone think of a sentence with a "*ly*" word in it that is an adverb?'

And after the predictable silence, a boy raised his justifiably tentative hand and answered: 'I ate my breakfast, muesli'.

Parts of speech are only what they are given their context. For example, in the sentence 'I am going on a fast for Lent', 'fast' is a noun. In the sentence, 'I run fast' it is an adverb. In the phrase 'the fast car' it is, of course, an adjective. So any cards displayed in classroom offering lists of adjectives are telling partial truths at best.

Here is a game to play to reinforce the parts of speech. It can be used to introduce the idea that I have sketched in the paragraph above: that the status of words is dependent on context. I have adapted this version of the game of Consequences from Brownjohn (1982), who calls it 'The Exquisite Corpse':

Give each player a strip of paper – half of a piece of A4 cut lengthways is perfect. Use the paper landscape rather than portrait fashion – that is, with the long sides at the top and bottom, not at the sides.

Ask the players to write in the top left hand corner either the definite or the indefinite article – 'The' or 'A'. Emphasize the technical language – 'article' etc. That language is part of what you are teaching here.

They then fold the paper to hide the letter, and put a dot on the paper near the edge. Make sure they don't fold the paper back, or dog-ear-wise, making a corner.

Then ask each player to pass his or her paper on to the person next to them. Everyone now writes an adjective where the previous player has put a dot. The procedure is the same as before: fold over the paper and put a dot, pass it on. Repeat for the following parts of speech, in the following sequence (I'm starting from the beginning again here):

article,

adjective,

noun,

verb (main verb – no 'ing' endings; any tense),

article + adjective (this pair should be done at one go),

noun.

Then open the papers. One possible problem: the verb may require a preposition after it.

Two examples:

The gruesome wall embraces the irrelevant antelope.

This next one has a verb that does require a preposition:

A sullen ape will dash [to, under, over, behind, before, beneath, within, … take your pick] the sexy atlas.

You can add an adverb after the final noun:

An indecent scrummage gestures at the correct antelope kindly.

Poetry

Stillman says that 'Poetry is, of course, verse – although not all verse is poetry. Poetry employs the same battery of techniques as verse, but it transcends verse in a way that has escaped definition … Poetry seems to partake of the miraculous … ' For some interesting and ultimately futile definitions of poetry, see Stephens 1990. In the context of definitions, note Grigson's comment, in which he quotes *Alice in Wonderland*: 'Why are we always asking for definitions of poetry? "No, no! The adventures first" said the Gryphon in an impatient tone: "explanations take such a dreadful time"'.

Punctuation

My friend Geoff Southworth was teaching in Preston in 1968. He told me that in that town, children did not say 'Yes Sir' or 'Yes Miss' but 'Sir yes' and 'Miss yes'. One day, a boy came to the front of the word queue (q.v.) with his exercise book. It looked an all right story but, Geoff told me, every word had a comma after it. 'Why has every word got a comma after it?' asked Geoff. The boy replied 'Sir, because I breathed'.

Do not fetishise punctuation, or contemporary rules about punctuation. They are always less use than they seem. This boy had been taught that you put a comma when you breathe, but not that this breathing is relevant as you read the work back to yourself, not as you write.

For more on the 'word queue', see the section with that title below.

Rhyme

No, it doesn't have to rhyme! Usually rhyme is not worth teaching to primary school children, except as a game. I know that this is quite unfair, because nearly all the poems that are written for children do rhyme, and also rhyme is part of the cultural definition of what poetry is: nursery poems and playground chants all rhyme. If a child does seem to be ready to use rhyme in a unforced way, and is keen to do so, point out that she does not have to make every end word rhyme. In children's writing, rhyme is like garlic or cayenne pepper: a little goes a long way. Suggest that in a short poem, the last word rhymes with a word used earlier. But there should be some reason for the rhyme, other than the coincidence of sound.

Sandy Brownjohn and Janet Whittaker (1985) have a good rhyme game: rhyme tennis. You serve rhymes to each other, scoring as in tennis. When one of the rhymesters fails to find a new rhyme, a point is lost.

HALF RHYME

Words that are close to chiming together, but don't quite. Wilfred Owen used half rhyme to powerful effect. See 'Futility' on p.153–4 for examples.

RIME

'Rime' is an old way of spelling rhyme, and is also, largely irrelevantly, hoar frost – frozen mist. But according to the National Literacy Strategy, rime is 'that part of a syllable which contains the vowel and final consonant or consonant cluster if there is one: *at* in cat; *orn* in horn … ' This last is not recognized by Stillman's *The Poet's Manual and Rhyming Dictionary* (1966), Gray's *A Dictionary of Literary Terms* (1984), John McRae's *The Language of Poetry* (1988), Philip Davies Roberts' *How Poetry Works;* or by two other authorities on my shelves, *Webster's Third International Dictionary*, or the *Shorter Oxford*. I have telephoned friends deep in the business of teaching poetry – brothers and sisters in the mystery – and they don't recognize it, either. I don't believe it – and even if, in some obscure spot 'rime' does mean this, what is the point? *What is the point?* Haven't we as teachers got enough paperwork to deal with without trivia like this? Please. For Heaven's sake.' Streuth. (*Exit* spluttering with rage.)

OK, it's a linguistic term, and the Strategy uses it in this sense. All my above comments still apply.

The Strategy (by the way) is guilty of a wonderful tautology: a couplet is '*two* lines of poetry which are *paired* … ' (my italics). It goes on to define tautology, rightly, as 'use of an extra word or sentence which unnecessarily repeats an idea'. It should have used its 'couplet' definition as an example.

Rhythm

'The pattern of recurrent alternation of strong and weak elements in the flow of sound and silence in speech'.

A problem with rhythm rests in the residual notion that the reading of a poem has to reflect exactly and crudely the tum-tee-tum of its supposed rhythm. If you read to children a poem with a strong regular metre and rhyme – 'I remember, I remember' by Thomas Hood, for example (see p.144), and ask the children to write a poem inspired by it, they may well avoid rhyme (having been told to do so – see last entry) but they will sometimes read their poems in the mechanical way I mean. They see this as reproducing a little versy list, end-stopping each line with a clunking pause before tum-tee-tumming the next line. To a sensitive adult ear this sounds awful, and children should be told that a poem is written in a language spoken by human beings to other human beings, and in the natural human speaking voice – but at its clearest best rather than casual conversational.

Simile

See 'metaphor'.

Stanza

Poems have stanzas like songs have verses.

Syllable (and syllabic count)

Syllables are useful in certain lessons, because having to count them takes the heat out of difficult subjects. A haiku has seventeen syllables, arranged by lines like this: 5,7,5. A tanka has 31, arranged like this: 5,7,5,7,7. A cinquain has 22, arranged like this: 2,4,6,8,2. There is no reason why a class of children should not invent their own syllabic poem, and give it a name.

Tanka

See 'syllables'.

Word queue

This is one of the most uneducational features of any classroom. It is that phenomenon we see where children queue, ostensibly, to get spellings checked, or to see if what they are doing is 'all right', or for a final assessment, or because they are 'stuck'. Why is this queue uneducational? For the following reasons:

First, the child in position three doesn't want to get to the front. S/he is there to take a little time out from work, and quite often can be caught ushering classmates ahead with a polite 'After you'. This child will stay in position three in the word queue as long as s/he isn't found out, or as long as s/he feels like it. While the teacher is concentrating on helping children at the desk, monitoring details like the child in position three is a low priority.

Second, the child at the end of the queue often presents a different problem. This child wants 'pterodactyl', 'accommodation' or even 'separate' and is unaware that Sir (in this case) can't help. What a disappointment that will be! After spending ten minutes, say, in the queue, this writer finds that s/he is no further forward in a piece of work that was enjoyable and fulfilling than s/he was when she joined the queue.

And what about the word books that are usually an integral part of the word queue system? One very organized teacher with whom I worked made sure every year that his class had a complete set of these, in some cases ranging from volume one to volume ten. Could the children spell all those words? Of course they could not.

Many years ago, some time in the early 1970s, I decided that the word queue was a waste of space and time, as well as a human shield preventing me from seeing part of the class. My first ploy was to not use my desk, but to work at the children's desks, moving round the room. The word queue became the word conga. Eventually I dispensed with the whole idea that children need to have spellings checked as they write. They don't, and to insist on doing that checking is a control mechanism on the part of the teacher.

A list of poems used in this book to help children to write

I note that there are no traditional English poems in Chapters 1–3 of this book. These subjects were beneath poetry, by and large, until the twentieth century. The inclusion of my own poems among poems by genii like Blake is meant nothing to imply anything about my poems' status; merely that I could reproduce them free, and they were useful for teaching some aspect of poetry.

WILLIAM BLAKE

I was angry with my friend (page 80).
Tyger Tyger (page 45).

RUPERT BROOKE

The great lover (page 92).

RICHARD CORBET

To his son, Vincent Corbet (page 86).

THOMAS HOOD

I remember, I remember (page 144).

GERARD MANLEY HOPKINS

Pied beauty (page 167).

WILFRED OWEN

Futility (page 153).
The chances (page 153).
The dead-beat (page 152).

PSALM 150

(page 170).

WILLIAM SHAKESPEARE

Full fathom five my father lies (page 189)

CHRISTOPHER SMART

For I will consider my cat Jeoffry (page 39).

JONATHAN SWIFT

We are five little airy creatures (page 56).

EDWARD THOMAS

If ever I should by chance grow rich (page 86).

Present day poems

JUDITH NICHOLLS

Name this child (page 63).

FRED SEDGWICK

Café at night (page 121).
Kelly Jane dancing (page 141).
Lullaby jazz for Daniel (page 175).
Riddle (page 55).
Match abandoned (page 116).
Mr Khan's shop (page 64).
Peasant wedding feast (page 121).
Things to do on the first day of the summer holidays (page 95).

References

The way to be esteemed Learned, is but only to have a Library, and to be able to Turn to the Indices.

Samuel Butler

Adelman, Clem (1987) 'The Art of Young Children' in Tickle (ed.) *The Arts in Education – Some Research Studies* London: Croom Helm.

The Art Book (1994:71) Phaidon.

Avery, Gillian (1994) *The Everyman Anthology of Poetry for Children* London: Everyman.

Barthes, Roland (1982) 'On Gide and his Journal' in Sontag (ed.) *A Barthes Reader* London: Cape.

Benton, Michael and Geoff Fox (1985) *Teaching Literature Nine to Fourteen* Oxford: Oxford University Press.

Benton, Michael, John Teasey, Ray Bell and Keith Hurst (1988) *Young Readers Responding to Poems* London: Routledge.

Brooke, Rupert *Collected Poems* (1932) London: Sidgwick and Jackson.

Brownjohn, Sandy (1982) *Does It Have To Rhyme?* London: Hodder and Stoughton.

Brownjohn, Sandy and Janet Whittaker (1985) *More Word Games* London: Hodder and Stoughton.

Byatt, AS (1988) 'Many poets, few good ones' *Guardian* 25 November 1988.

Causley, Charles (1974) *The Puffin Book of Magic Verse* London: Penguin.

—— (1975) *Collected Poems* London: Macmillan.

—— (1996) *Collected Poems for Children* London: Macmillan.

Chambers, Aidan (1986) interview by Philippa Hunt and Elizabeth Plackett *The English Magazine* Autumn 1986.

Clayton, Martin (1992) *Leonardo da Vinci: The Anatomy of Man. Drawings from the Collection of Her Majesty Queen Elizabeth II* Boston: Little, Brown.

Corbett, Pie and Brian Moses (1986) *Catapults and Kingfishers: Teaching Poetry in Primary Schools* Oxford: Oxford University Press.

Cotton, John and Fred Sedgwick (1996) *Two by Two* Ipswich: JDDJ Press.

Crossley-Holland, Kevin (trans.) (1979) *The Exeter Book of Riddles* London: Penguin.

Crossley-Holland, Kevin and Lawrence Sail (eds) (1999) *The New Exeter Book of Riddles* London: Enitharmon.

Eagleton, Terry (1978) *Criticism and Ideology: A Study in Marxist Literary Theory* London: Verso.

Gaarder, Jostein (1995) *Sophie's World* London: Phoenix.

Gardner, Helen (1972) *The New Oxford Book of English Verse 1250–1950* Oxford: Oxford University Press.

Gray, Martin (1984) *A Dictionary of Literary Terms* London: Longman.

Grigson, Geoffrey *The Private Art* London: Allison and Busby.

Hardy, Thomas (1969) *Collected Poems* London: Macmillan.

Heaney, Seamus (1966) *Death of a Naturalist* London: Faber and Faber.

—— (1996) *The Spirit Level* London: Faber.

Heaney, Seamus and Ted Hughes (1982) *The Rattle Bag: An Anthology of Poetry* London: Faber and Faber.

Hourd, Marjorie L (1949) *The Education of the Poetic Spirit* London: Heinemann.

Hughes, Ted (1960) *Lupercal* London: Faber and Faber.

—— (1967) *Poetry in the Making* London: Faber.

—— (1970) *Crow* London: Faber.

—— (1977) *The Poetry and Voice of Ted Hughes* London: Caedmon (tape recording).

Hull, Robert (1988) *Behind the Poem: A Teacher's View of Children Writing* London: Routledge.

Larkin, Philip (1988) *Collected Poems* London: Faber and Faber.

—— (1983) *Required Writing: Miscellaneous Pieces 1855–1982* London: Faber and Faber.

Lee, VJ (ed.) (1987) *English Literature in Schools* Milton Keynes: Open University Press.

Lindop, Grevel (1981) *The Opium Eater: A Life of Thomas De Quincey* London: Dent.

Longland, Jack (ed.) (1983) *Young Writers 24th Year: Award-winning Entries from the 1982 W H Smith Young Writers' Competition* London: Heinemann.

Mackenzie, Suzie 'Enemy Within'. Interview with Helen Dunmore, *Guardian*, 26 August 1999.

MacLeod, Isaebail and Terry Freedman (1995) *Wordsworth Dictionary of First Names* London: Wordsworth.

McRae, John (1998) *The Language of Poetry* London: Routledge.

Morgan, Margaret (ed., in association with Suffolk County Council) (1988) *Art 4–11: Art in the Early Years of Schooling* Oxford: Basil Blackwell.

Newland, Mary and Maurice Rubens (1984) *Some Functions of Art in the Primary School* ILEA.

My Hand is Elastic: Award-winning Entries from the 1993 W H Smith Young Writers' Competition (1993) London: Macmillan.

Opie, Iona and Peter (1955) *The Oxford Nursery Rhyme Book* Oxford: OUP.

Opie, Iona and Peter, and Maurice Sendak (1992) *I saw Esau: The Schoolchild's Pocket Book* London: Walker.

Orwell, George (1961) *Collected Essays* London: Mercury Books.

Owen, Wilfred (1964) *Collected Poems* (ed. C Day Lewis) London: Chatto and Windus.

Panichas, George (1977) *The Simone Weil Reader* New York: McKay.

Partridge, Eric (1992) *A Dictionary of Traditional First Names* London: Wordsworth.

Pirrie, Jill (1987) *On Common Ground: A Programme for Teaching Poetry* London: Hodder and Stoughton.

Plath, Sylvia (1981) *Collected Poems* (edited and introduced by Ted Hughes) London: Faber and Faber.

Popa, Vasco (1978) *Collected Poems* Manchester: Carcanet.

Raine, Craig (1979) *A Martian Sends a Postcard Home* Oxford: Oxford University Press.

Redgrove, Peter (1987) Interview in *The Poetry Review* London: The Poetry Society.

Roeves, Emily (in progress) *Versions of Goethe.*

Roberts, Philip Davies (1986) *How Poetry Works: The Elements of English Poetry* London: Penguin.

Sainsbury, Robert (1978) *Robert and Lisa Sainsbury Collection*: Catalogue for the exhibition for the opening of the Centre, April 1978, Norwich: University of East Anglia.

Sedgwick, Fred (1989) *Here Comes the Assembly Man: A Year in the Life of a Primary School* Basingstoke: Falmer.

—— (1994a) *Collins Primary Poetry* London: Collins.

—— (1994b) *Pizza, Curry, Fish and Chips* London: Longman.

—— (1994c) *Personal, Social and Moral Education* London: David Fulton.

—— (1994d) 'Me and the rest of the world' *Montessori Education* Vol 6 No 1.

—— (1997) *Read My Mind: Young Children, Poetry and Learning* London: Routledge.

—— (1999a) *Blind Date* Ipswich: Tricky Sam! Publications.

—— (1999b) *Thinking About Literacy: Young Children and their Language* London: Routledge.

—— (1999c) *Shakespeare and the Young Writer* London: Routledge.

—— (2000a) *Themes for Poetry* Dunstable: Belair.

—— (2000b) *Forms of Poetry 1* Dunstable: Belair.

—— (2000c) *Forms of Poetry 2* Dunstable: Belair.

—— (2000d) *Jenny Kissed Me: An Anthology of Poems About Love* Birmingham: Questions Publishing Company.

—— (2000e) 'When the inspectors call' *Montessori International* Winter 2000.

Sedgwick, Dawn and Fred (1996) *Art Across the Curriculum* London: Hodder and Stoughton.

Spenser, Herbert (1929) *Education, Intellectual, Moral and Physical* London: Watts.

Stephens, Meic (1990) *A Dictionary of Literary Quotations* London: Routledge.

Stevens, Wallace (1965) *Selected Poems* London: Faber.

Stillman, Francis (1966) *The Poet's Manual and Rhyming Dictionary* London: Thames and Hudson.

Styles, Morag, Eve Bearne and Victor Watson (eds) *The Prose and the Passion: Children and their Reading* London: Cassell.

Summerfield, Geoffrey (1970) *Junior Voices, the fourth book* London: Penguin.

Thomas, Dylan (1952) *Collected Poems* London: Dent.

Thomas, Edward (1981) *The Collected Poems of Edward Thomas* Oxford: Oxford University Press.

Thomas, R S (1993) *Collected Poems 1945–1990* London: Phoenix.

Townsend, John Rowe (1979) *Modern Poetry: A Selection* Oxford: Oxford University Press.

Tunnicliffe, Stephen (1984) *Poetry Experience: Teaching and Writing Poetry in Secondary Schools* London: Methuen.

Vernon, P E (1970) *Creativity* London: Penguin.

Whiting, Roger (1992) *Leonardo: Portrait of the Renaissance Man* London: Barrie and Jenkins.

Willans, Geoffrey and Ronald Searle (1958) *Down with Skool* London: Collins.

Wilson, Anthony (1998) *The Poetry Book* London: The Poetry Society.

Yeats, W B (1983) *Collected Poems* (ed. Richard J Finneran) London: Macmillan.

Index

acrostic poems 114
Adelman, Clem 139
adjective, 193–4
adverb, 193–4
alliteration 95, 112, 167, 169–70, 191
anger, writing about 78
Arnold, Matthew xvii; 'Creep into thy
    narrow bed' 187
article, 194
Arts Council 182
assonance, 170, 191
attention 102, 139
Auerbach, Frank, on observation 3
Auden W H, on naming cats 61; on
    playing with language 69; 'The More
    Loving One' 189
Austen, Jane 18
autonomy and young children 42, 165
Ayres, Pam 158

B*witched (popular music group) 156
Barker, Dale Devereux (artist) 53
Barthes, Roland 81
Benn, Aphra xviii
Bing Xin (Chinese poet) 158
Browning, Elizabeth Barrett xviii
Bennet, Elizabeth (character in Jane
    Austen's *Pride and Prejudice*) xviii
Blair Government xvi
Blake, William xvii, (on observation) 3
    'The Tyger' 45; 'I was angry' 78–9, 181
Britten, Benjamin, early memories 147
Brooke, Rupert, 'The Great Lover' 36, 91–4
Brownjohn, Sandy 14, 83, 185, 187–8
Brueghel, Pieter the elder, 'Peasant
    Wedding Feast' 121–2
Causley, Charles xx, 165
Chagall, Marc, 'The Walk' 123

Cherokee chant about names 60
Chipperfield, Sophie (teacher of poetry)
    53, 100–4
choice, as educational 188
Christmas, writing at, 171–5
cinquains 115, 191, 197
class poems and group poems, infants
    composing them 94, 97–8, 140, 148
cliche 59; preventing the possibility of 117,
    142–3, 158–9, 161, 191–2
Coleridge, Samuel Taylor xvii, 158
common sense, the dreaded, 78
competition and writing xiii, 53, 165–6
computers xx, 77, 113
control (as opposed to autonomy) 42
Corbet, Richard, 'To his son, Vincent
    Corbet' 86
Crossley-Holland, Kevin, and riddles
    55–6; and the Anglo-Saxons 182
computers 185
cummings, e e 68

Daily Mail 188
Darwin, Charles 5
da Vinci, Leonardo, sketchbooks xix; on a
    cat's eyes 39, 41
death, children writing and talking about
    105–8, 132, 160
democracy (poetry as a democratic subject)
    xiii, 17, 71, 97
de-mystifying poetry 97
Dickens, Charles, naming in *David
    Copperfield* 60
Donaghy, Michael 186
drafts and drafting xiii, 53, 126, 140–1, 192
drawing and writing xiii, xxi, 12–13; anger
    drawings 81–2, 135; bicycle drawings
    28–32; cat drawings 43–4

Duffin, John, 'We weren't going anywhere' 122
Dunmore, Helen, on observation 4

elegies, children writing them 105–8
Eliot, T S 77
endings, writing about 96–7
erasers and why they should be banned from classrooms 30
essays, teaching the writing of them 60
expectations, high, as encouraging 18
experience, first-hand 20, 157–8

Faith, Adam 187
First World War poetry 151–6
free verse, as imprisonment xix
Freud, Sigmund, on play, children and creativity 139

Gardner, Helen, on paucity of women poets in the *Oxford Book of English Verse 1250–1950* xviii
Genesis Chapter 2, on naming 59–60
Giacometti, Alberto 30
Goethe, Johann Wolfgang von xix; last words 28
Golden Treasury, paucity of women poets in xviii
Graham, Billy, and guilt 187
grammar xiii, xvii, 42, 68
Grey, Thomas, 'Elegy' 186, 190
group poem, juniors 157

haiku 54–5, 111, 114, 192, 197
Hardy, Thomas, 'Afterwards' 3–4; 187
Heaney, Seamus, 'Blackberry-picking' 21; 'The Rain Stick' 33
Henri, Adrian, 'Tonight at Noon' 142
Herbert, George 18; 'Love bade me welcome' 187
history 151
Holub, Miroslav, 'The Door', 5–6; on science and poetry 8, 60
Hood, Thomas xviii; 'I remember, I remember' 144, 181, 196
Hopkins, Gerard Manley, 'Pied Beauty' 167, 188
Hopper, Edward 123–6, 129
Hughes, Ted 8; *Crow* 26; 'Hawk Roosting' 50, 53
hypotheses, children on art 132
information and communication technology xx

Jegede, Emmanuel 129
Joyce, James, *Portrait of an Artist* 164

kennings 15–17
Klee, Paul, 'Lines into Knowledge' 13

labelling, treating very young children as writers 42
Larkin, Philip 26, 46; 'Midsummer Waking' 50; 'Days' 177, 187–8
Lawrence, D H, on 'the essential quality of poetry' 139
learning from children's writing 9–10, 125–6
Letterland folk, as images that children ignore 134
limericks, dubious 182
literacy, the Literacy Strategy and the Literacy Hour xv–xvi, xviii, xix–xx, 112, 183, 196
Longfellow, H W 187
Lowry, L S 134
luck, writer's 118
lullabies, children writing 175

Machine, the (metaphor for the mechanisation of society and education) xvii, 122, 139
mathematics 35
melodrama in children's writing 53
memory and children's writing 144–7
metaphor 21, 33, 35, 42, 159, 192
metaphysical truths xvii, xxi
Meynell, Alice xviii
Molesworth, Nigel 186
Montessori education 129–30
Montessori, Maria 130
More, Hannah xviii
multilingualism xvi
multiracialism xv
Murray, Les 168

National Curriculum 17, 53
Nicholls, Judith, 'Name This Child' 63–4
noun, 193–4

object lessons 3
observation xiii, chapters 1 and 2, 41, 55, 120, 158–60
obsessions, children's, as subjects for writing 99–100
OFSTED xxi, 4–5
onomatopoeia 140

Opie, Iona and Peter, *Oxford Nursery Rhyme Book* 112
Orbison, Roy 96
Orwell, George 159
oxymorons 117, 158
Owen, Wilfred xviii; 'The Dead Beat', 'The Chances', 'Futility', 'Dulce Et Decorum Est' 151–6; 181; 196

PSME (Personal, Social and Moral Education) 60
Picasso, Pablo, 'Mother and Child and Four Studies of her Right Hand' 125, 127; on being like a child 158
Pirrie, Jill (writer on children and poetry) 171
Pitney, Gene 96
plagiarism 77
Plath, Sylvia, 'Mirror' 104
Platt, Michael (dancer and dance teacher) 53
play 139–41, 145, 189
Poetry Society 182
Popa, Vasco, 'Give me back my rags' 78
postcards, used for stimulating writing 119
Pound, Ezra xiii, 158
praising children 11
prayer 166, 178
prepositions, teaching them 150–1, 193
prose 59–71, 158
provisionality, children's acceptance of in writing 9, 14, 24
Psalm 150, 170
publishing children's work xx
punctuation xiii, xvii, 183, 195
puritanism 139

questions to help children writing 88, 104, 145, 159; of God 164, 174; stupid 165

Raine, Craig, 'A Martian Sends a Postcard Home' 167
Rattle, Simon xvi
Redgrove, Peter 5
repetition 145
rhyme and children's writing 10, 26, 46, 112, 195–6
rhythm 196
Richard, Cliff 96, 187
riddles 54
rime 196
risk-taking in children's writing 50
Robbe-Grillet, Alain, 192
Rossetti, Christina 181

Rubens, Maurice 12

Sail, Lawrence, and riddles 56
Sainsbury Centre 53
St John's Gospel 28
St Luke's Gospel 174
Sassoon, Siegfried 151
Sawyer, Tom, and his Aunt Polly 60
science and poetry 5, 8, 35
secretarial skills xiii, xvii, 97
self-esteem, improving it through writing 100–4
Shakespeare, William, *Anthony and Cleopatra* xviii; *A Midsummer Night's Dream* 17–19; *King Lear* 22; *Cymbeline* 105; *Romeo and Juliet* 117; Sonnets 18 and 19, 181; Sonnets 18, 129 and 130, 187; 'Full Fathom Five' from *The Tempest* 189; 'I'll follow you' and 'You spotted snakes' from *A Midsummer Night's Dream* 189
similes, helping children to make them 11, 21–4, 33, 35–7, 42, 140, 159, 192
Smart, Christopher xviii; 'My Cat Jeoffry' 39–41, 81; 181
Smith, W H, Young Writer's Competition 53, 124
Sorhaindo, Imani (African Caribbean artist-writer) 130
speech bubbles 42
spelling xiii, xvii, 42, 68, 183
Spenser, Herbert, on observation 3
stanza 197
Stevens, Wallace, 'Thirteen Ways of Looking at a Blackbird' 14–15
structures (value as prison cells in helping children to write) xix, 88, 148–9
Swift, Jonathan (vowels riddle) 56
syllabic poems 114–16, 197
syllables, 192, 197

tanka 115, 197
Tardios, George 79
technology 35
Thatcher Government xvi
Thomas, Dylan 168
Thomas, Edward, 'If ever I should by chance grow rich', 86; 'And you Helen' 88; 188
Thomas, R S, and the Machine xvii
Topping, Angela, 'My Best Friend' 84–5

Van Gogh, Vincent, 'Sunflowers' 111, 134; 'Cafe at Night' 121

verb, 42, 193
Vico, Giambattista, and metaphysical
    truths xxi
vocabulary book, as useless 42

Weil, Simone, on attention and truth 102,
    128, 139
Word on the Street (popular music group)
    156–7
word processing xiii, xx, 27, 37, 77
word conga 198

word queue, as useless 42, 197–8
Wordsworth, William, 'Tintern Abbey'
    190
writing corner 106

verb 193–4

Yeats, W B, 'To a Squirrel at Kyle-na-no'
    48, 187–8; 'The Wild Swans at Coole'
    189
Yoruba culture 129